THEOLOGY AND THE CURE OF SOULS

By the same author

THE MEANING OF SIN   *Fernley-Hartley Lecture*
JESUS THE SON OF GOD
'WHEN I DIE.'   *Pamphlet*

THEOLOGY AND THE CURE OF SOULS

AN INTRODUCTION TO PASTORAL THEOLOGY

by

FREDERIC GREEVES
Principal, Didsbury College, Bristol

The Cato Lecture of 1960

WIPF & STOCK · Eugene, Oregon

Wipf and Stock Publishers
199 W 8th Ave, Suite 3
Eugene, OR 97401

Theology and the Cure of Souls
An Introduction to Pastoral Theology
By Greeves, Frederic
Copyright©1960 Methodist Publishing - Epworth Press
ISBN 13: 978-1-4982-8051-8
Publication date 1/28/2016
Previously published by Epworth Press, 1960

Every effort has been made to trace the current copyright owner
of this publication but without success. If you have any information
or interest in the copyright, please contact the publishers.

PREFACE

SOME creative artists have said that they are indifferent to the possibility of their work being seen; others of us who write books find it necessary to cherish the hope that a few people will read what we have written. I should like to think that, in spite of its title, some lay Christians will read this book, for it discusses a pastoral ministry in which all Christians may share, and a theology that belongs to all Christian living. I have tried to confine more technical theological matters to Chapter Twelve and a few parts of Chapter Three.

Although much is said about Methodism, I hope that some Christians of other denominations may be sufficiently patient to exchange my Methodist currency for their own.

I have said much about Methodism for two reasons. Firstly, because I am a fourth-generation Methodist minister, who has lived for over fifty years in a 'manse', his father's or his own. Great as is the debt that I owe to Christians in many denominations, it is only possible to speak with confidence about what one knows from within; that is one of the sad consequences of disunity. Secondly, it was the expressed wish of Fred J. Cato that the Lectures which he endowed should 'encourage and foster fraternal relations with Methodism of other lands'. If I have, to a small degree, succeeded in helping my Methodist brethren, at home and abroad, towards understanding of ourselves, I shall be very glad; if I have unintentionally misrepresented the 'people called Methodists', I shall be very sorry, but I am sure that nobody else will be blamed for my faults.

These words must be written before my wife and I set forth to enjoy the generous hospitality of the Methodist Church throughout Australia, about which our predecessors have told us. We know that there, and in other countries which kindly invite the Cato Lecturer and his wife, we shall learn and receive far more than we could ever hope to give. I express my sincere gratitude to the Trustees of the Cato Foundation who have honoured me with this invitation. I am also grateful to J. Alan Kay, Editor of

The Preacher's Quarterly, for permission to make use of material contributed to the first volume of that journal, and to former students and other friends who have encouraged me to write about the theme of this book.

FREDERIC GREEVES

Biblical quotations are taken from the *Revised Standard Version.*

CONTENTS

Preface v

Part One

THEOLOGY AND PASTORAL CARE

1. THE CURE OF SOULS 3
   - The meaning of 'cure of souls' 4
   - The scope of pastoral care 8
   - The early Church and the cure of souls . . 13
   - The plan of this book 16

2. THE PASTORAL OFFICE TODAY 18
   - Sociological changes 21
   - Psychology and spiritual direction . . . 23
   - Contributory hindrances to a pastoral ministry . 26

3. THEOLOGY AND THE CURE OF SOULS . . . 32
   - Contemporary attitudes towards theology . . 32
   - The function of theological statements . . . 34
   - Some attempts to divorce theology and experience . 40
   - The interdependence of theology and experience . 46

Part Two

FROM DOCTRINE TO PASTORAL CARE

4. THE DOCTRINE OF THE TRINITY AND THE CURE OF SOULS 53
   - The Triune God 54

Theological inquiry and Christian living	. .	57
'Three-in-One and One-in-Three'	. . .	58
'Mysterious Godhead, Three-in-One'	. . .	63

5 FROM THE DOCTRINE OF FULL SALVATION . . . 67
    Justification and sanctification 68
    Perfect love 74
    Assurance 79

6 FROM BELIEF ABOUT THE NATURE OF THE CHURCH . 84
    The Church and the gospel 85
    Many truths about the one Church . . . 88
    The holy and sinful Church 91
    The Church and the world 95

Part Three

FROM PASTORAL EXPERIENCE TO THEOLOGY

7 FROM LISTENING TO PEOPLE 99
    Creator of heaven and earth 102
    The sacred and the secular 107
    Man in the image of God 109

8 FROM CARING FOR SINNERS 113
    The sin-sick 113
    Sin against God 118
    Law and gospel 122

9 IN SICKNESS AND IN HEALTH 126
    Suffering 127

CONTENTS ix

Health 133
Death 137

Part Four

THE PRACTICE OF THE CURE OF SOULS

10 THE MINISTRY OF THE WHOLE CHURCH . . . 143
    The whole Church 143
    'Lay' pastors 148

11 THE MINISTRY OF THE MINISTER 152
    A professional ministry 152
    Spiritual direction and responsive counselling . . 157

12 THE MINISTRY OF THE THEOLOGIAN . . . 161
    Note A—Fundamental doctrines . . . 167
    Note B—Methodist doctrine 170

13 SHEPHERDS WHO ARE ALSO SHEEP 174

    Index 179

PART ONE

THEOLOGY AND PASTORAL CARE

CHAPTER ONE

THE CURE OF SOULS

THIS book ranges over a somewhat wide territory; it raises many issues, without fully exploring them; it asks questions which it does not profess to answer; in places, it makes dogmatic statements without producing the evidence upon which they are based. It may, therefore, be wise to explain, in this opening chapter, the scope and purpose of the inquiry which is to be undertaken.

Firstly, something must be said about what I have not attempted to do. This book is not a survey of the art or technique of pastoral care; although much will be said about very practical matters, I shall not presume to tell ministers or laymen how to do their work. Neither will there be found in these pages an attempt to provide a summary of pastoral theology, about some of the major Christian doctrines little will be said; no particular doctrine will be fully examined.

This book is primarily concerned with the relationship between Christian doctrine and pastoral care. Although, as will be suggested in this chapter, 'pastoral care' is a concept which is as relevant to preaching as to individual personal contacts, and is a responsibility of all Christians, not only of ministers, it will be possible to make only fleeting reference to some aspects of this 'care'. The fact that attention will be focused upon the place of theology within the pastoral office means that many other no less important pastoral requirements will receive scant mention.

Concentration upon the place of doctrinal teaching in the cure of souls implies neither that this is the sole task of the Church nor that theology is the only thing needful for its fulfilment. Conviction that all men, both as 'sheep' and as 'shepherds', need Christian doctrine, to a far greater extent than is now commonly recognized, does not involve the belief that doctrine is all that they need. If wearisome repetition is to be avoided, these limitations in the scope of this book must be made clear at the outset.

In selecting the title, I have deliberately risked misunderstanding and even antipathy, for it seemed better to run that risk than to conceal my purpose. It is precisely because 'theology' has come to suggest to many people what is far removed from the daily life of Everyman, and because the term 'cure of souls', in spite of its honourable history, has never been popular in some Christian traditions and has now become somewhat archaic, that the title may serve to indicate that I am trying to correct some common misconceptions. In this chapter we shall be concerned with the term 'cure of souls'; the two following chapters will have more to say about 'theology'.

I. THE MEANING OF 'CURE OF SOULS'

In spite of the fact that both words, 'cure' and 'souls', are susceptible of false interpretation, the description of pastoral care as 'the cure of souls' is one for which no alternative is readily available. We must, therefore, look more carefully at each of these words in turn. In the preface to his invaluable book, *A History of the Cure of Souls*, John T. McNeill pointed out that the word 'cure'

has something like the range of meaning of the Latin *cura* from which it comes. The primary sense of *cura* is 'care' and it is readily applied either to the tasks involved in the care of a person or thing, or to the mental experience of carefulness or solicitude concerning its object. Occasionally the former direction of meaning is further specialized to signify 'healing', or the means by which healing is effected. It was natural that the Latin Church should employ the expression *cura animarum* in such a way as to comprehend these variations of the meaning of *cura*, and it is in this comprehensive sense that the term 'cure of souls' has come into common use in English.

Perhaps the German word *Seelsorge*, for which there is no single-word equivalent in English, conveys this manifold meaning even more clearly. In *sorge* (as in *cura*) there is a reminder of deep concern and of the actions to which that concern leads, as there is also in our English word 'care'; but in *cura animarum* and in *Seelsorge* are found the thought of 'healing', which belongs to our word 'cure', rather than to 'care'. That is why 'care' of souls is no adequate substitute for 'cure' of souls.

Another phrase once current among Christians is still occasionally used: 'a passion for souls'. In this phrase is something of the intensity of solicitude that belongs to *cura animarum*, but too often this 'passion' has referred only to the conversion of the unbelieving, and not, also, to the whole area of pastoral care. We still need, I believe, a distinctive term for the pastoral attitude and function which can remind us that Christian care, like the love of God Himself, must be for all men, everywhere and in all matters, and which never allows us to forget that the Church's purpose, which is that of Christ Himself, is the healing and health that come from God.

But if there is no substitute for 'cure', is not 'souls' a word which conceals rather than illumines the nature of pastoral care? There is much force in this objection. So deeply engrained in our common thought is the concept of the total separation of soul from body, a concept which has much in common with Greek thought, but is irreconcilable with the outlook of both Old and New Testaments, that we may well be loath to speak of 'souls', and prefer to talk of 'persons'. There are, however, several reasons why it would be unwise for us to be content to talk about 'the cure of persons'.

In the first place, we should then be tempted to escape from the difficult duty of understanding the psychological outlook of the Scriptures. As is now widely recognized, neither Old nor New Testament offers us either a trichotomy (a threefold division into soul, spirit, body) or a dichotomy (a twofold division into soul or (spirit) and body).[1] That fact does not imply that the Hebrew and Greek terms translated by those English ones have little significance; it implies, rather, that all their meanings are meanings about the *wholeness* of man.

In this respect biblical psychology is nearer to much present-day psychology, and especially to the psychosomatic approach of much modern medicine than are many professedly Christian views of human nature. To that extent it ought to be easier for us than it was for our immediate predecessors to avoid thinking of human beings as 'souls' imprisoned in bodies from which they need to be rescued. A passion for souls that involves indifference to the mental and physical needs of men and women should, by now, be as psychologically absurd as it is spiritually disastrous. In this way, as in not a few other ways, scientific knowledge has made it easier for us to read the Bible, which is not itself a scientific work.

But that is not the whole story. For the emphasis upon the mind-body relationship, which is expressed rather than explained

---

[1] Th. C. Vriezen, *An Outline of Old Testament Theology*, pp. 201f.

in the current term 'psychosomatic', has made it more difficult, rather than more easy, for us to find any content in the word 'soul'. The fact that we cannot point to any part of man and label it 'soul' should not, it might be imagined, trouble those who have recognized that we cannot find a part of man to be described as 'mind' (as distinct from 'brain'), but who are aware that we must continue to speak about mental (psychic) processes as well as about physical ones, so that we must refer to 'minds and bodies'. Yet the situation is not so simple, for it is by no means difficult to imagine that we can manage quite well without the notion of 'soul'. I believe that we can in fact do so if we reject or ignore the existence of God and man's relationship to Him.

To quote from an admirable article in *A Theological Word Book of the Bible*,[2] it is 'as the creature of God [that man] is a living soul marked out for a special relationship and destiny (Gen 2^7, 1^{26}, etc.)'. In this respect, as in all others, the interest of the Scriptural writers in man is in man as he is created and redeemed by God, in man as he comes from and is destined for God.

We need the word 'soul', therefore, in order that we may be reminded of man's relationship to God and of his need for God. The twofold approach that is described by the term 'psychosomatic', by which the interrelationship of mind and body is kept in view, must for the Christian believer, become a threefold approach. We must no more think of soul as existing independently of body than of mind as divorced from body; if 'a passion for souls' leads us to treat ourselves and other people as disembodied spirits, we must refrain from such a 'passion'. It is because 'body, mind, soul' represents a unified totality, that pastoral care extends to every aspect of man's manifold existence; it is because by forgetting what 'soul' represents we misconceive the nature and needs of both body and mind, that the cure of souls has its distinctive place alongside physical and psychiatric healing.

This discussion about the term 'cure of souls' began with reference to the Latin word *cura*, and it is important to recall that the primary meaning of *cura* is 'care', with 'healing' as its secondary meaning. We are constantly in danger of thinking that pastoral care, whether by individuals or by the Church as a whole, can itself heal men and women. The French surgeon who wrote on the wall of his operating theatre, 'I dressed the wound, but

---

[2] 'Spirit', p. 234.

God healed it', was giving expression to a fundamental truth. The non-believer will prefer to speak of 'Nature' as the healing power; the believer attributes all health and all life to God. In the distinctive work of the cure of souls it is of especial importance that this should never be forgotten, yet it is both obvious and mysterious that God, who alone is the source and sustainer of life, has given to human beings very great (but not unlimited) responsibility for the welfare, and for the very existence, of themselves and of each other. It is only as we fully recognize this fact that the urgency of pastoral care is fully appreciated; it is only if we are confident that all life and health depend upon God that we can believe in the human ministry of a cure of souls.

Amongst many reasons for the partial neglect of the Church's pastoral responsibility (others of which will be referred to later) there is one which requires emphasis at this point. A sincere, yet false, reverence for God may lead to the notion that men ought not to interfere in God's work. Misconceptions of this kind have often caused Christians to hinder the work of physical and mental healing, or to stand aside from political and social activity, in order that all may be left to God. A similar attitude can influence the devout in relation to the cure of souls. Examples of this mistaken attitude will call for closer attention in later pages, and we shall see that they have reference to both the beginning and the development of Christian life. Although extreme forms of quietism may be rare, there are many Christians who are somewhat suspicious of any form of preaching which involves more than repetition of Biblical language, lest 'the human element' should misinterpret the word of God, and who are distrustful of any human interpretation of the Word of God.

It is, however, in relation to the instruction of converts, the discipline of Church members, the human share in the divine work of repentance and forgiveness, and the whole part that men must play in both their own and their neighbours' spiritual growth, that hesitation and even fear are most common. It is (as we shall see) strange that such apprehension should exist in Methodism, in view of its beginnings.

These fears are not wholly groundless. We know that, early in its history, the Christian Church lapsed into trust in humanly-won merit, that a great edifice of salvation-by-works was built upon a foundation of by-grace-alone, that clerical supremacy and ecclesiastical power crept in, even where least to be expected, and we have much evidence of how humanistic a professedly Christian Church can become. A. Raymond George has wisely reminded Methodists that 'we need still to maintain our traditional view that it is possible to be an Arminian without being a Pelagian'. Who would claim that we have always done so? Only as we recognize that, in all His ways, God demands human co-operation, can we recognize these dangers without being paralysed by them.

In this, as in all things, we must learn from Christ. Little imagination is required to see how foolish and ineffective His ministry would have been had it been the purpose of God to save men against their will and without their willing response. When we learn from Jesus that God's purpose was exactly the reverse, we can recognize this same purpose in all God's ways. It is God who provides man with food, yet starvation faces the world as an imminent danger; it is God who heals, yet millions suffer and die for want of human aid; it is God who speaks the Word of life, 'but how shall they hear without a preacher?' So, too, it is Christ who is the Shepherd of our souls, yet there are lost sheep which are not found, and found sheep which are lost, because some of those who care for the sheep are hirelings rather than shepherds. There is no escape from the cure of souls.

II. THE SCOPE OF PASTORAL CARE

Having seen a little of the meaning of the term 'cure of souls', we pass on to a preliminary survey of the *scope* of this task. In so doing, it may become a little clearer that this 'cure' involves *healing*, but we shall nevertheless best approach this inquiry by considering an alternative description of the cure of souls— namely, 'pastoral care'.

The pastoral or shepherd image has profound significance for our comprehension of Christ's own work and, therefore, also for our understanding of the mission which He entrusts to His Church. In *The Significance of the Cross*,[3] F. W. Dillistone has remarked that our Lord did not (as we might have expected) describe Himself as Redeemer, Saviour or Deliverer; He spoke of Himself, rather, as Shepherd. Dillistone reminds us of the rich Old Testament content of this image. 'No simile is more often

[3] Pp. 26ff. I am indebted to Dr Dillistone in this and the following paragraph.

employed in reference to the exodus of the Children of Israel from Egypt than that of a shepherd leading forth his flock.' Psalmists and prophets use this imagery, as they look back to the former deliverance and forward to the new redemption; Ezekiel denounces the false shepherds and declares the promise of God that He will become their Shepherd (Ezk 34); Isaiah (40) and Jeremiah (23³, 31¹⁰) describe the Shepherd who is to come.

It is with all this (and much more) in mind that we must hear our Lord's own description of Himself as the Shepherd. Whilst it is to John 10 that our minds naturally turn when we think of Jesus as the Shepherd, we must not forget how frequent are occurrences of this same image in the Synoptic Gospels (cp. Mk 6³⁴, Lk 12³², Mt 15²⁴). Most of all, when the image of the Shepherd occupies our attention as we contemplate the work of Christ and the ministry of His Church, we must recall (as Dillistone suggests) Christ's quotation from Zechariah in Mark 14²⁷. The Shepherd is to be 'smitten'; the Good Shepherd lays down his life for the sheep.

Only as we see the pastoral work of Christ Himself as part of the meaning of His whole work of redemption can we rightly comprehend both the primacy of His own pastoral work and the character and scope of the Church's pastoral ministry. The Church has no pastoral office of its own; if Christians are called to be shepherds, they are only under-shepherds. Just as there is only one High Priest, so there is only one Good Shepherd; yet to belong to the Church of Christ is to be involved in His priestly and His pastoral work. It is only thus that we dare speak about 'Christian pastors'; it is from this standpoint alone that we can see the all-embracing extent of the pastoral task.

Even more foolish than the alleged distinction between a preaching and a teaching ministry is the supposed contrast between pastoral work and evangelism. It is the lost sheep whom the Shepherd seeks; it is the scattered sheep whom He would gather in. Although there is all the difference between those who are in and those who are outside the fold, those who are without are His 'other sheep' (Jn 10¹⁶). Only because that is so, can Jesus pray that they may become one flock. If the evangel calls the sheep home, it does so precisely because they *are* sheep, and because they will be 'at home' in the Shepherd's fold and among the Shepherd's flock.

Whilst, then, we shall in later chapters be much concerned with the care of those who are within the Church, we must never allow ourselves to forget that the shepherds' deepest concern is for those who are furthest away. It is only as evangelism is motivated by pastoral compassion that it can be truly Christian evangelism; it is only shepherds who care about the sheep outside who can begin to understand the needs of the sheep within.

Let us now, for the time being, turn from this vivid imagery of sheep and shepherd, and from the Scriptures themselves, to see how a few Christian pastors have conceived the scope of pastoral care. John T. McNeill, in *A History of the Cure of Souls*, has illustrated this theme with such a wealth of historical detail that I can only hope that any reader who has not studied that book will soon do so. I select four writers in different periods, to whom McNeill refers: Augustine, Bucer, Baxter and John Wesley. About the last two of these I propose to say a little more than McNeill has space to say.

Here, first, is Augustine's description of the tasks to be done:

Disturbers are to be rebuked, the low-spirited to be encouraged, the infirm to be supported, objectors confuted, the treacherous guarded against, the unskilled taught, the lazy aroused, the contentious restrained, the haughty repressed, litigants pacified, the poor relieved, the oppressed liberated, the good approved, the evil borne with, and all are to be loved. [4]

We may miss from this list a close association of pastoral duty with evangelism, but careful examination will show that this omission is more apparent than real, and that the catalogue, if not exhaustive, is suggestive.

It has become a platitude, in conversation about pastoral care among those of us who stand within the protestant, evangelical tradition, to say that we need someone to do for our day what Martin Bucer (d. 1551) and Richard Baxter (d. 1691) did for theirs. McNeill points out that Bucer in his treatise, *On the True Cure of Souls and the Right Kind of Shepherd*, describes his work in terms of Ezekiel 34[16]: 'I will seek the lost, and I will bring back the strayed, and I will bind up the crippled, and I will strengthen the weak, and the fat and the strong I will watch over.'[5] This

---
[4] Augustine, *Sermo*, CCIX; cited, J. T. McNeill, *A History of the Cure of Souls*, p. 100.
[5] Bucer apparently used a text which is similar to that used by *R.S.V.*, from which I quote.

passage, which vividly reminds us of Christ's own description of His mission, and of His quotation from Isaiah 61 (Luke 4^{18f}), is the basis of Bucer's fivefold analysis of the cure of souls: 'to draw to Christ those who are alienated; to lead back those who have been drawn away; to secure amendment of life in those who fall into sin; to strengthen weak and sickly Christians; to preserve Christians who are whole and strong, and urge them forward in all good'.

Ezekiel's reference to the divine care for 'the fat and the strong', and the last two items in Bucer's classification, draw our attention to an aspect of pastoral concern which must not be obscured by the sense of responsibility for the 'lost sheep' of which I have previously spoken. This same emphasis is found in Baxter's *The Reformed Pastor*.

In a chapter on 'The Oversight of the Flock' there is a section entitled 'The Nature of this Oversight'. Baxter begins where we have begun, with evangelistic pastoral duty: 'We must labour, in a special manner, for the conversion of the unconverted.' He then summarizes the 'building up of the converted' under four heads:

(a) The immature, including those who 'though of long standing, are yet of small proficiency or strength'.
(b) Those who 'labour under some particular corruption, which keeps under their graces, and makes them a trouble to others and a burden to themselves'.
(c) 'Declining Christians', who have fallen into some scandalous sin or lost their zeal.
(d) 'The strong'.

About 'the strong' Baxter comments that they specially require 'our attention, partly to preserve the grace they have; partly to help them in making further progress; and partly to direct them in improving their strength for the service of Christ, and the assistance of their brethren; and, also, to encourage them to persevere, that they may receive the crown' (Chapter 2, Section I.3.iv).

Few better descriptions of the need to 'watch over the fat and the strong' can have been provided by a Christian writer. Whilst, in order to keep our pastoral perspective, it is necessary to stress the place of evangelism within the cure of souls, it is equally essential to emphasize the need for continued care of the converted if the evangel itself is not to be misconceived. Two related facts about the gospel may serve to illustrate this point: it is an offer of *life*, and it is a call to a *growing* life.

Life is one of the fundamental biblical concepts, by no means limited to the Johannine writings or to explicit use of the term 'life' itself. The new birth, the new creation, adoption and (rightly understood) justification all point to the fact that in Christ, through the Holy Spirit, a Christian is summoned to and fitted for a totally new existence. But this life, like all life, involves growth. This life, like natural, physical life, must give place to death unless life be sustained, and extension of life involves growth; when we cease to grow we begin to die. Nobody understood this need for growth better, and no Church leader ever sought more fully to make room for this truth in the structure and pattern of Church life, than did John Wesley, who is the last of our four examples of interpreters of pastoral duty.

It has unfortunately happened that Wesley's emphasis upon the beginning of Christian life (shown in his Sermons and, even more specifically, in his *Journal*) has led to partial forgetfulness of his passionate concern about growth in Christian life. H. Lindström, in *Wesley and Sanctification*, has shown how Wesley combined with belief in the reality of instantaneous conversion an insistence upon gradual development. I am sure that Lindström is right when he says (p. 105): '. . . the fact that Wesley also sees salvation as a gradual development is a most prominent element in his conception of salvation, and indeed in his thought generally'. Much of the evidence for the truth of this statement, provided by Wesley's theological writings, has been summarized by Lindström and need not be repeated here, but to recognize the full import of this emphasis upon growth we should need also to examine in detail nearly every feature of the early Methodist Societies.

In *A Plain Account of the People called Methodists*, Wesley wrote:

They were built up in our most holy faith. They rejoiced in the Lord more abundantly. They were strengthened in love, and more effectually provoked in every good work.

In the forthright document which is usually known as 'The Larger Minutes', Wesley instructed his preachers about their duties to the members of the Societies in plain words which left no room for suspicion that the converted could be left to their own devices. He would have them visit each house, take each member aside for loving but penetrating examination and counsel, catechize the children, and entrust religious responsibilities to the head of each household. By his insistence upon attendance at and adequate care of the classes, by his provision for the regular testing of the ministry and by the whole developing structure of the Societies and of the Conference, Wesley sought to ensure that all that was humanly possible should be done that the Great Shepherd's care of the flock might be not hindered, but served.

I have only observed one occasion upon which Wesley spoke of a cure of souls, but it is typical of his outlook. In a letter (25th March 1772) he wrote: 'O what a thing it is to have a *curam animarum*! You and I are called to this; to save souls from death; to watch over them as those that must give account! If our office implied no more than preaching a few times in a week, I could play with it: so might you.' That comment by one of the most assiduous and effective of all Christian preachers, whose successors have always laid a primary emphasis upon preaching, is a memorable remark. Can it be said that Methodism, as it has developed, has retained, in its teaching or in its practice, this indivisible association of evangelism with pastoral care, of the new birth with Christian growth?

III. THE EARLY CHURCH AND THE CURE OF SOULS

Wesley would have told us that all that he believed and taught about pastoral duty was learnt from Scripture, although, in this respect as in all other matters, he would have added that 'reason' and 'experience' confirm Scripture. It is necessary for us to observe, in the New Testament records, that from its first beginnings, and perhaps especially in its first years, the Christian Church combined thorough care of those inside with ceaseless concern for those outside the Church.

A general survey of the Acts of the Apostles and the Epistles would furnish a great variety of examples of the pastoral theology and practice of the New Testament Church, especially if this were studied against the background of the Old Testament and of other records of later Judaism. (John T. McNeill has shown that the rabbis may rightly be termed 'pastors'.) There are a few valuable chapters on this subject in McNeill's book and there is incidental treatment in many commentaries upon particular New Testament books, but I am not aware of any full-length study of the pastoral element in the New Testament writings as a whole; it may be hoped that some scholar, with the needful critical scholarship, will provide us with a study of that kind. Here, only two illustrations of the field to be examined can be offered: the work of Paul in particular and the general catechetical teaching of the early Church.

(1) In this matter, the teaching of Paul is illuminating both in its totality and in specific instances. McNeill, in a few pages (80-5), has provided a broad survey of Paul's total message and work, and in so doing he has demonstrated the truth of Martin Schlunk's comment that Paul 'possessed the gift of the cure of souls [*Seelsorge*] in outstanding measure and employed the art with wonderful mastery'. Christians, and especially those who are deeply involved in the pastoral work of the Church, can strengthen their own appreciation of the fact that the missionary-apostle was a pastor-apostle by reading the Epistles with this in mind, and by noting, on almost every page, explicit and implicit references to the needs of the flock. These are found even in the midst of profound theological argument.

An example of a specific instance of Paul's pastoral approach is provided by his letter to the Philippians. We cannot doubt that Paul wrote many letters such as this, letters which, we may be confident, he did not write as documents for posterity. Here, in Philippians, is an example of a minister's letter to his congregation, a type of correspondence which many readers of this book will often have practised; but how different is Paul's letter from ours! The way in which his doctrine and his pastoral exhortation are bound up with each other is superbly illustrated in this Epistle, but that will concern us more particularly in the next chapter; what concerns us now is that in its short space it provides example after example of Paul's care for the churches, of a pastoral love that is never sentimental or censorious, of clear, firm, yet gentle teaching about Christian morality, prayer, endurance and faith. Here babes in Christ are being taught how to grow.

(2) My other example of ways in which the pastoral teaching in the New Testament may be studied is provided by evidence of definite catechetical teaching in the early Church. Archbishop Carrington's study, *The Primitive Catechism*, has been followed by a number of other works which have endorsed and illuminated his pioneer work. The most detailed and clear summary of the

evidence is provided by Essay II in E. G. Selwyn's, *The First Epistle of Peter*; and G. Phillips, in *The Transmission of the Faith*, has worked out some of the implications of this scriptural teaching for the contemporary Church in diverse countries and cultures. This material will be familiar to many readers, but because of its importance for the whole theme of this book, I must briefly describe it.

A comparative study of the Epistles (especially Romans, Colossians, Ephesians, 1 Peter, James and Philippians) suggests that there was a reasonably precise scheme or pattern of teaching by which those who received the gospel were instructed in the faith. In reducing this scheme to the following outline I have somewhat simplified, but not (I believe) in any way distorted the picture. The pattern of teaching seems to have been as follows:

I. Entry into the new life at Baptism
   (*a*) Its basis: the Word (gospel)
   (*b*) Its nature: rebirth, new creation, etc.

II. The negative implications of the new life:
   Vices and errors that must be 'put off'

III. The positive implications of the new life:
   (*a*) Faith and worship
   (*b*) Duties and virtues
   (*c*) Facing 'crisis' (watch, pray, stand fast)

Whilst I do not suggest that we must presume the existence of an official texbook for the training of catechists, a copy of which might one day be discovered, I am wholly convinced by the argument that it was on this type of instruction, and from these points of view, that the first Christians were 'built up in our most holy faith'. G. Phillips, in the book mentioned above, has shown how this same pattern of teaching can be directly adapted to the needs of modern men in many different environments. Other facts suggested by this 'scheme' will be mentioned in later chapters of this book, and the reader may care, from time to time, to turn back to this summary. For the moment I only wish to draw attention to it as powerful evidence of the part that the cure of souls played in the beginnings of the Church. In particular, it should be noted that the first item in the list is teaching about the entrance into the new life.

That observation brings us back to one of the main themes of this chapter: the relation between evangelism and pastoral care. Of course there is a difference between *kerugma* and *didache*, between what is proclaimed and what is taught; of course there is a difference between seeking the lost sheep and caring for those that have been found. And it is indeed true that nobody is 'saved' by teaching or by theology. But everyone who receives the Gospel needs to be helped to discover what it means; all who are 'born of water and the Spirit' need to learn what that birth means. Hence, a primary and fundamental part of the responsibility of the Church is to make plain (or, as plain as the mysteries of God can be made) what God *has already done*.

The man who is 'born again when he is old' needs, as truly as one who was baptized in infancy, to discover the meaning of the gracious work of God that has already been done for and in him. Because grace is always prevenient, because God always takes the initiative, true Christian living requires us to find out what He has done, as well as what He seeks to do. This is a task that cannot be completed in this world, but it is one that must begin and continue, if the believer is to continue and grow in the faith. Perhaps one of the best ways of thinking of the cure of souls is to view it as the Church's responsibility for mutual help in discovering the meaning and the implications of the new life in Christ.

IV. THE PLAN OF THIS BOOK

Even this brief examination of the meaning and scope of the cure of souls may have served to show how comprehensive is the pastoral responsibility of the Church; a full study would be concerned with all aspects of Christian life, individual and corporate. It will be obvious that this book cannot attempt to survey the whole of this vast territory, and it may be of some help to the reader if our future course is mapped out.

In the next chapter we shall consider more carefully the place of the cure of souls in the contemporary Church, and, in so doing, we shall try to discover some of the reasons for the partial neglect of this responsibility. It will be suggested that the weakening of pastoral care has been partly due to forgetfulness of the pastoral character of theology; and so, in Chapter 3 the relationship between theology and pastoral need will be examined. That will conclude our discussion of the three nouns in our title, *Theology and the Cure of Souls*, which has begun in this chapter, and will bring Part One to an end.

Two further tasks then become necessary, if the argument of the first three chapters is valid: (i) a consideration of Christian doctrine itself from the pastoral angle, and (ii) a practical study of how the pastoral office may be fulfilled. In Parts Two and Three, dealing with the first of these two tasks, there will be offered, not the full-scale pastoral theology which many of us hope will one day be given to the Protestant Churches, but a few illustrations of what such a work would involve. (The method by which the chapters on this subject are divided into two parts will be explained on p. 50). In Part Four, dealing with the second of our two tasks, a few comments will be made upon the practical implications of what has previously been said; we shall look at some of the diverse 'ministries' within the cure of souls. In this last Part, special attention will be paid to a fact which should be borne in mind throughout earlier chapters: the pastoral work of the Church is not the exclusive responsibility of the ordained ministry. There is a sense in which every Christian is called to be a shepherd, but this can only be rightly understood if we recall (as the concluding chapter will do) that every Christian is also a 'sheep.'

CHAPTER TWO

THE PASTORAL OFFICE TODAY

THOSE who owe all that is best in their lives to the pastoral ministrations of the Christian Church, and especially those who have also had the privilege of sharing in that ministry, can best recognize that all is not well with the pastoral office today. (The assertion that those outside see most of the game is on most occasions fallacious; it is particularly untrue with respect to the work of the Churches.) I am very anxious not to exaggerate the position, and therefore I do not depend only upon my own observation, but also upon the wider and deeper experience of many Christians of many denominations who, in private and in public, have expressed the concern which I share. Some of the occasions for this concern must be briefly mentioned before we search for reasons for that weakened emphasis upon the cure of souls which is characteristic of much Church life today.

In the Protestant Churches of England (I cannot, here or elsewhere, speak with knowledge about the Roman Church), it has become widely true that if men and women (within or without the Church) turn readily to a Christian minister for individual spiritual counsel, they most often do so because they are attracted by the personality of the man rather than because he is the minister. Ministers who move to a new church or parish have to win confidence in a way that no medical physician needs to do; the doctor may lose the confidence of his patients, but they do not begin by doubting or failing to recognize that he is a doctor.

In the United States (so far as my opportunities for observation and reading permit a generalization) the situation is rather different. I was impressed wherever I travelled in that country by the fact that people still think of the minister as a 'counsellor'. Even to visit the church office of an American minister is to be reminded of the professional character of the pastor's work. Am I wrong in thinking that the problem which faces ministers in North America is that they are primarily consulted as psychologists? In print and in conversation many of them have expressed their concern about this matter; they have pointed out to British ministers who are tempted to envy their situation that a crowded office or consulting room does not of necessity provide evidence of a fully pastoral ministry. When people turn to the ministry for counsel, that is a matter for gladness; but what if they turn for psychological rather than for spiritual counsel? What if their very eagerness to be helped with needs of one kind forms a hindrance to the satisfaction of needs of a deeper kind. I think that many thoughtful Christians in the United States are recognizing that there are deficiencies in their form of the cure of souls, even if those deficiencies differ from ours.

In England, it is not uncommon to meet devoted Christian ministers who confess that many weeks, even years, pass with little private conversation with men and women about the things of God. This is a state of affairs which our Christian fathers would have deemed unthinkable. Moreover, in many denominations, and even in Methodism which has historically emphasized the pastoral function of the laity, there are countless examples of Churches where no systematic teaching is given outside the pulpit, where no opportunity is provided for mutual care in bible-study groups, fellowship meetings and the like. For many years we have been watching children departing from our Sunday schools, and young people from our youth organizations, with a minimum of knowledge about the faith of the Church in which they have sojourned. When trouble overtakes even long-established members, it often finds them almost as ill-equipped with the Christian verities as their pagan neighbours; when the verbal attacks of unbelievers assault them, many Christians discover that they have nothing to say; when moral judgements, in private or public matters, need to be made, multitudes of professed Christians have to rely upon intuition or the conventional moral beliefs of their neighbours.

Of course, this brief description is not a total picture. It is, indeed, the many exceptions to the situations we have noted which bring the need into focus. I am quite sure that a factual study of Church life would show that wherever the kind of failure which I have mentioned is strikingly lacking, the absence is due to some form of sustained pastoral work, and I believe it would be found that this pastoral work has a doctrinal basis. That this is no purely individual opinion may be illustrated from an incident in the British Methodist Church a few years ago.

The Conference, as a delayed response to a memorable presidential address by W. F. Howard, appointed a Committee bearing the strange title: 'The Committee for Direction in Things Spiritual'. The title appeared strange, both because modern Methodists do not now take kindly to the word 'direction', and also because it appeared that the committee had no work to do which could easily be recognized as 'practical'. After the passing of a few years, it may not be improper for the convenor of that Committee to say that he found its first meeting a memorable experience. Men and women of very diverse shades of opinion and types of responsibility gathered to converse, with no agenda other than the instruction of Conference to consider the deepest spiritual needs of the Church. Out of what at first appeared to be a welter of confused ideas, there quickly appeared a clear and unanimous conviction that, over and above all the needs of contemporary Methodism, was the need to discover for our generation what John Wesley discovered for his: ways through which Christians might be 'built up in our most holy faith'. In particular the need was recognized for pastoral and moral theology with which Methodists could feel at home.

Some of the vision which came to us in that committee, which we never succeeded in communicating to the Church as a whole, has been recaptured in English Methodism by a movement among laymen. So far as I know, the men who in growing numbers are influenced by this movement have little contact with the lay movements which are one of the most hopeful signs in many European churches (see Chapter 10). It is noteworthy that all such stirrings of conscience and zeal are characterized both by pastoral concern in general and by a particular realization of the distinctive place of Christian theology within the pastoral office. One may be allowed to wonder whether the ordained ministry of more than one denomination has recognized fully how widespread are these movements of thought among the laity.

Yet it remains true, not only that the world outside the Church is increasingly failing to recognize the pastoral function of the Church, but also that, over wide tracts of the Church's own life, that ministry is largely dormant and the place of doctrine within it is scarcely recognized. We turn, therefore, to consider some of the many reasons for this situation.

I. SOCIOLOGICAL CHANGES

Changes in the pattern of society inevitably profoundly affect the Church's mission, not because the essential nature of that mission varies, but because hindrances to, and opportunities for, its fulfilment are modified. This is a fact which is well known and much discussed in reference to evangelism; has comparable consideration yet been given to the effect of social change upon the Church's pastoral work?

In many parts of the world, the more obvious points of contact between the Church and the world have been removed or are rapidly passing away. In some countries great material prosperity, in others relative material progress combined with the development of a Welfare State, reduce almost to non-existence the *direct* corporate activity of the Church in the relief of basic physical needs. Both the charity and the ignominy of the soup kitchen are passing away; a swiftly growing army of social workers has largely replaced the amateur service of visitors 'from the Church'. The development of both lower and higher education has made obsolete the general educational work which was formerly provided within and by the Church. Commercial entertainment and the money to purchase it have largely displaced the function of the Churches as providers of recreation. In these and other ways the Church no longer meets a host of needs in the lives of its members which it was still meeting even less than fifty years ago; it no longer has these easily recognized and appreciated points of contact with people outside its membership.

Too often attempts are made to swim against the tide. Christians are still encouraged to work in well-intentioned but inexpert forms of social service which are judged to be 'Christian' because they are run by Church organizations, rather than to seek membership of skilled voluntary or professional 'secular' organizations. Third-rate entertainment is still offered as a bait to attract people from the 'pleasures of the world'; somewhat pathetic attempts are made to 'give young people something to do', whilst the world outside the churches is full of tasks waiting to be done.

But although unrealistic attempts to deny the fact that 'the world' can (and should) perform most of these tasks better than the Church may, for a time, win adherents, the success thus won is itself a failure. The concept of the Church as an organization which does the world's work for it may be defended by a doctrine of the Church, but such doctrine is irreconcilable with that of the New Testament. It is, in fact, a total misunderstanding of the nature of the Church; for the Church is inevitably doing the world's work just because Christians are in the world—or ought to be. Although communities of Christians must ever be ready to offer themselves, their buildings and all their resources for any care of men's bodies and minds that cannot be undertaken in co-operation with non-believers, Christians should never be the first to encourage this kind of segregated effort. Those who are not against Christ are for Him, and therefore they are potential colleagues of His people.

In prosperous countries and in Welfare States there is still plenty of room for voluntary social service, but there, and even in parts of the world where such need is still immense, it will increasingly be met by governments and by non-ecclesiastical agencies. The monstrous suggestion that Christians should hold up the progress of physical and cultural betterment, either because it is dangerous to be rich or because poverty and pain provide opportunities for Christian ministry and incentives to Christian faith, only requires mention to be rejected. It is always right to feed the hungry, but we should be grateful if less occasion is given for the temptation to encourage 'rice Christians'.

This changing social pattern must be both welcomed and understood by Christians. Have we yet adjusted ourselves to it? Many practical questions about the amount of time to be devoted, by both ministers and laymen, to activities within the church, and about the nature of such activities, urgently need to be answered. At the very least, it should be recognized that there is a growing opportunity for concentration upon the evangelical-pastoral work of the Church, undistracted by many of the calls that once clamoured for attention. Can it be said that we are always using this freedom rightly, that we care for 'souls' more adequately because we have (within the churches themselves) less to do for 'minds and bodies' than had our fathers? Now that an army of trained social workers minister to needs which formerly demanded the time of ministers of religion, are we more fully engaged in the cure of souls?

Such questions are forced upon our attention by the contemporary situation. Answers that take the form of generalizations are almost certainly false; each Christian, and each local church, must take stock. There is not a little that must cause disquiet. Often it appears that when men do not ask us for bread, we have little to offer them. No longer can we pretend that *only* fully-committed Christians love their neighbours, nor can we cherish the illusion that men and women will be won for Christ wholly by our love for them, although they may well be kept from Him by our lack of love. This changing world, at which we have briefly glanced, compels us to ask afresh: What is the *distinctive* character of the cure of souls?

II. PSYCHOLOGY AND SPIRITUAL DIRECTION

The second influence that has affected the pastoral work of the Church is the modern growth of psychiatry and, especially, of popular interest in psychiatry. At this point I must emphasize that I should be very distressed if any reader were to imagine that I were seeking to under-estimate the importance of psychiatric work, or even suggesting that Christian ministers and laymen should fail to be intensely interested in it and, in some ways, involved in it. It is, however, because of the remarkable developments in this sphere of medicine, and the enormous possibilities for the welfare of mankind which a more fruitful treatment of mental illness offers, that we need to rescue ministers of religion, the medical profession and patients from the non-professional practice of psychiatry which, in some quarters, is in danger of totally eclipsing truly spiritual direction. Some justification of this statement must now be offered.

In the first place, psychiatry has now passed beyond the stage at which it was possible for a non-professional to gain adequate knowledge. Chatty talks based on superficial 'introspection', the half-digested study of popularized Freud, casual observation and (not to mention living persons) the type of pre-scientific psychology associated with pioneers such as William James, belong to the past. Whatever may one day prove to be the truth about the mind-body relationship, the so-called psychosomatic approach is at least as likely to show that all mental illness requires physical remedy as it is to show the reverse. The day has long since arrived when only a fully medically trained psychiatrist can be trusted to be in charge of such work, however many workers trained in other sciences are needed as auxiliaries.

Is the Christian minister (for in this matter we are obviously concerned particularly with the ministry) to work as an auxiliary to the psychiatrist? This appears to be what many people, including a few medical men, believe his function to be. But let us examine what this idea involves. Not a few psychiatrists and psychologists welcome ministerial co-operation as an aid to mental health, even though they do not accept the truth of the beliefs which Christians proclaim. Is this a point of view which we, as Christians, ought to tolerate and encourage, however flattering it may be to think that we are wanted? Is not a use of religion as a way of mental health, in spite of the fact that religious beliefs are judged to be purely 'mythological' (in the sense of being untrue), a way of reducing Christianity to magic, a way which we should have to repudiate even if we were persuaded that it would produce beneficial results?

Other medical men who welcome ministers as auxiliaries do so because they clearly recognize the limitations in their own work. This is a very different point of view, but it is often misunderstood. Surely Christian psychiatrists and other doctors of this type want the minister's help precisely because he is not a psychiatrist, but a minister? They want him because (even though they are believers) they have neither time, nor (they would modestly say) the gifts and training, to do what the minister exists to do. Unfortunately, it is probably true that the vast majority of the medical profession (even if we exclude those who are atheists) does not know very clearly what it is that the minister really can 'do'. Is this wholly the doctors' fault? It is not always easy to discover what kind of specialists we modern ministers are.

David Stafford-Clark, a distinguished psychiatrist, has written: '. . . any success achieved by psychiatry in straightening out a tangled mind, in helping a man to think more clearly and honestly, must inevitably help him also to open his mind and his heart to God—if he so chooses.'[1] The evangelistic-pastoral ministry is to help him towards this choice. Moreover (although psychiatrists differ greatly in their attitude to this as to all other matters) a very considerable part of psychiatric opinion is opposed to the deliberate exercise of influence by the psychiatrist upon the moral and religious beliefs and attitudes of his patient. What kind of 'direction' the Christian pastor should give in these matters is a

---

[1] *Christian Essays in Psychiatry* (ed. P. Mairet), p. 23.

difficult problem which must await discussion until Chapter 11, but it can at least be asserted here that all Christian pastors must be primarily concerned about the moral and religious life of those whom they are called to help. Both because some psychiatrists think it wrong to interfere in these matters, and because some who do deal with them do so from points of view which are opposed to Christian belief, we need consultants in the moral and religious life. Who can fulfil this function if not the minister? The task is more than sufficient for any man's time.

There is, however, a much deeper reason why psychiatric and spiritual counselling functions must not be confused, and it is well put by Stafford-Clark in the same context:

The contribution which Christianity can make to problems arising out of the therapeutic situation is fundamental. It can reconcile the inevitable conflict between loving and hating which psychotherapy may bring up into consciousness. It is important to realize that psychiatry by itself cannot really do this; it is not *in itself* a source of inspiration, nor can it provide a substitute for moral values or obligations, and it is only inviting trouble to pretend that it can.[2]

Psychiatry is providing fresh opportunities to Christian pastors, both because it is releasing many people from that mental darkness into which no consciously-received help can come (however deep may be the unsearchable influence of divine grace), and also because it is beginning to help us towards better understanding of many of the needs which the Christian gospel satisfies. It is helping those who lack their Lord's own knowledge of what is 'in' men to know more about them. We must not over-estimate that help; psychology and psychiatry are young sciences, and their exponents as yet agree in little. Neither must we under-estimate the help that is offered; that is why every Christian, and especially every minister, must seek to familiarize himself with the more agreed psychological findings. But to play at practising psychiatry, even under the cover of association with an expert, is not only to court disaster, but to abandon the very needs which psychiatry helps to expose. There are very many people (though never enough) who are seeking to help those with troubled minds; but how few there are who have time to talk with them about God!

The way back to a specifically pastoral ministry is a long one.

[2] Ibid., p. 23.

It is tempting to say: 'Here is one point of contact that is not lost but increasing; we will persuade people to come for the Church's ministrations thinking them to be psychiatric in character, and then we will lead them where we want'. They will come in great numbers; if we have a bit of showmanship we can perhaps keep them coming; and if we have some real knowledge we can perhaps help them. But would not this subterfuge be but a new version of other ways of inviting men to God under false pretences, a modern counterpart of the meal-plus-evangelism, or of the youth-club with religion carefully concealed—methods which have proved their worthlessness? Do we not make it harder, rather than easier, for men and women to seek and find the health which is often very different from what by many would be called full physical and mental health, the health which God makes possible? Why do so many of us seem to be almost ashamed of being the kind of specialist that we are supposed to be?

When a minister or Christian lay worker says, 'I am not interested in theology', we should, perhaps, do him the courtesy of treating his comment as a jest. But what kind of a joke should we think it to be if a pilot remarked, 'I am not interested in aeronautics', or if the doctor told us, as we entered his surgery, 'Of course medicine is not in my line'? It is essential that every Christian who cares for his neighbours should seek such understanding as a layman can acquire of all that is being done by those who professionally serve the mental and physical needs of mankind; and, it need hardly be added, in so far as Christians participate in those professional services they are as truly serving their Lord as is any minister of religion or lay pastoral worker. But even if we hesitate to speak of theology as a science, we need to rediscover the truth that the Christian ministry is a profession as well as vocation.[3]

III. CONTRIBUTORY HINDRANCES TO A PASTORAL MINISTRY

Considerable space has been devoted to the general influence of social change and to the particular effects of the growth of interest

---

[3] Further remarks about a 'professional ministry' are made later (pp. 152ff). In what has been written above I do not wish to deny that some individuals may have the gifts for expert work as both psychiatrists and ministers, although it seems probable that in future they will also require full medical qualifications. There is however a difference between an 'ordained psychiatrist' (a concept depending upon our interpretation of the meaning of ordination) and the substitution of normal pastoral functions by psychiatric ones.

in psychiatry, because I believe that these are major factors in the present situation. A number of other reasons for the partial decline in the Church's pastoral ministry require briefer mention. Just as those changes which we have already considered are developments which are not to be regretted, but which, rightly handled, provide fresh opportunities for the cure of souls, so most of the tendencies now to be mentioned are full of opportunity as well as of danger.

1. First there is the growing emphasis that is laid, in many spheres, upon the corporate aspects of human life. Politically, economically, educationally and in other ways it is groups of people, rather than individuals, who dominate thought and compel action. At its worst, this is a move towards collectivism, towards the submerging of the individual in the group (large or small), and towards the horrors of complete totalitarianism. It would appear, at times, as though mankind were being driven to that goal by irresistible forces. Can anything but the Christian faith conquer that fear or, indeed, prevent the fear from becoming an actuality?

The strength of this collectivist tendency, by no means confined to the political arena, can only be appreciated when we recognize its moral appeal. If collectivism is evil, individualism is even more evil. To lose the individual in the mass is to deny one of the basic convictions of Christian belief; but to injure the many in concern about the individual, whether one's self or another, is to deny the whole of Christian faith. It is not surprising, therefore, that, to multitudes of men and women throughout the world, a narrow, individualistic type of religious interest appears to be highly immoral in comparison with care for the people, the nation, the race. One of the by-products of this movement of thought is the belief (or suspicion) that the Church's pastoral care encourages selfishness. Shocking as it may sound to Christian ears, many would consider that the shepherd who abandoned the ninety-nine for the one lost sheep was neglecting his duty to the flock, and that the lost sheep should welcome his own destruction provided that the flock were safe. Yet it was a simple, devout Christian who cried, 'Lord, I don't want to be saved out of a damned world!' And did not Paul say something very akin to this when he thought about his kinsmen according to the flesh? (Rom 9[3]).

If pastoral work involved, as to many it seems to involve, the deliverance of individuals from the society of which they are part, the guidance of them to a self-centred religious 'experience' in this world and to a private enjoyment of God in the next world, then it would indeed compare unfavourably with the self-forgetting service of those who toil and suffer and die for what they believe to be the good of mankind as a whole. That this is not the pastoral aim may seem obvious to readers of this book; that it appears thus to very many sincere people today must be recognized. Whether this is a true or false description of pastoral care depends upon the *theology* that belongs to the cure of souls.

2. Another hindrance to pastoral activity today, and one which particularly illustrates the way in which what is in itself good can have harmful by-products, is the emphasis, within the Church itself, upon the evangelism of the unconverted.

One of the healthiest signs in the life of all denominations today is a revival of evangelical concern, a concern which is by no means limited to those about whom the word 'evangelical' is unhappily employed as a classifying term. If we once more recall New Testament metaphors, we may say that there is growing eagerness to be fishers of men, but that sometimes this is accompanied by diminished attention to the task of tending the lambs and feeding the sheep. If we allow ourselves to play with the metaphors a little, we may say that in the miracle of divine grace the 'fish' very rapidly turn into 'lambs', that most of them take a long time to grow into 'sheep', and that the sheep never cease to need a shepherd's care.

Those of us who have opportunity to know the men who are offering for the Christian ministry today cannot but be impressed by their evangelical zeal; they often put to shame those of us who recall our own younger days. Is it unfair to say that some of them find it more difficult to care for the flock of Christ, and that this is why some become frustrated and disappointed when the routine of Church life becomes familiar to them? Part of the remedy for this tendency (if it exists) lies in the realization that there is no gap between evangelistic and pastoral work, a point that has already been sufficiently stressed. But perhaps we must also realize that pastoral work calls for spiritual maturity. Is it of some significance that Christ sent Peter immediately to fish for men, but that it was only 'after thou art converted' that Peter was commissioned to strengthen the brethren? It was only after the bitterness of denial and the miracle of his meeting with the risen Saviour that Peter was charged with the care of the sheep. This does not mean that every evangelist must deny his Lord before he can become a pastor! Does it not mean, however, that so far from pastoral work being a lesser responsibility than evangelism, it is one that makes even greater demands?

3. Within the Church and outside it, pastoral work is also hindered by the fact that there are many Churches. I believe that this divided state of Christendom has a special bearing upon prevalent attitudes to the theological aspect of the cure of souls. How can there be 'a pastoral theology' when in fact there are many theologies?

There are people who say that denominational and other Christian disunity does not trouble 'the man in the street', or that, if it appears to do so, that is only because he is making an excuse for his own lack of religion. I wholly dissent from that view, which is, I believe, an instance on the part of Christians of wishful thinking. It is not unusual to hear unbelievers say, when the Church's doctrine is mentioned, 'Which Church are you talking about?' Moreover, a great many Christians, including many ministers, are, I am sure, so aware of the conflicts in theological thought today that they consciously or unconsciously abandon hope of finding their way through the battleground to a theology that they can use as pastors.

This is part of the sin of the Church, that the truth of God is hidden behind the divisions among Christians; this is *our* sin. For that reason I am anxious not to minimize the gravity of this hindrance to the Church's task. It is true that theological differences are no longer wholly parallel with denominational divisions, even if they ever were, which is doubtful. Most of the diverse currents of theological belief run across the denominations, but our denominational allegiances make it hard for us to recognize this fact or to come to a common mind. Protestants are afraid of certain truths which they could believe, because Catholics hold those beliefs firmly, and I often seem to see the same tendency among Roman Catholic theological friends—for example, in reference to justification through faith. The emphases of one denomination tend to be exaggerated and made exclusive in order to preserve ecclesiastical identity. This tendency we see most clearly in some of the smaller sects, but Methodism also has much to learn about this danger in reference to its particular emphases (see Note B, p. 170). We cannot expect to have a wholeness of Christian doctrine in a divided Church.

Yet grave as this divided doctrine of a divided Church is, by the mercy of God the work of God is not wholly stultified. There *is* one Lord, one Faith. Not only is there far more agreement among Christians of all denominations about many fundamental aspects of the Christian Faith than is generally recognized, but also, because the truth of God, is many-sided, some differences represent not contradictions but partial glimpses of the truth. Unhappily, we Christians, and perhaps especially those of us who have special theological responsibility, tend to advertise our divergences rather than our agreements.

About all that has been said in the last few paragraphs more must be said later, but the fact that there are 'many theologies' adds point to other facts that have emerged in this chapter. All the contemporary tendencies at which we have glanced—sociological, psychological, and those that have to do with current attitudes to life in general and religion in particular—present us with questions which are ultimately theological. It is what we believe about God, and about all things in the light of God, that ultimately determines our response to the situations and to the points of view that I have mentioned. If God is God, then the answers to all the most significant questions that men ask are answers about God.

We therefore cannot shrink from the full implications of two facts: theology matters supremely, and there are different theologies. These cannot all be completely true, although (as has been said) the real contradictions may be fewer than at first sight appears. This means that God can be misrepresented; and it follows that His children, who need His care, may be hurt by false theology. This is a distasteful truth, but it is in harmony with every other fact about human life. Man has it in his power to hurt or to help his fellow men; why should we think that pastoral care is immune from either possibility? If God has laid upon the Church the task of evangelism, so that many will never hear the gospel because we fail them, why should we hesitate to recognize the full implications of the fact that He has charged His Church with the care of those who receive the gospel? The theological task is only part of the pastoral responsibility, but it is the part with which these pages deal. Before we can travel further in our inquiry about this task, we must notice some of the hindrances to the cure of souls which are themselves theological. Not only are both the kind of pastoral care that is offered and the results of that care in large part consequent upon the kind of theology which the Church believes and teaches, but the degree to which the Church *believes in* the cure of souls is partly determined by its theology.

CHAPTER THREE

THEOLOGY AND THE CURE OF SOULS

IT would be very difficult to make a fair assessment of contemporary attitudes towards theology, even if the inquiry were limited to one country. In England the situation is complex. On the one hand, we see a small minority attending the churches, and we find that very many Church members are theologically confused, sometimes theologically indifferent; on the other hand, we discover an insatiable desire to ask theological questions. Every preacher is accustomed to the remark, 'We don't want theological sermons', but this comment is often made in the midst of dogmatic theological statements by the commentator. A theological student who, during his time in college, was not conspicuously interested in the study of theology, wrote, soon after beginning work in an industrial area: 'It's theology wherever you go; in the pubs, the factories, the open-air and the youth clubs, it's theology all the time.' A theological tutor is inclined to suspect that it is only in theological colleges and in some congregations that one must sometimes struggle to maintain interest in doctrine. At the risk of making false generalizations, a few observations upon the present situation must be attempted by way of introduction to a study of the relation between theology and pastoral work.

I. CONTEMPORARY ATTITUDES TOWARDS THEOLOGY

(a) There are many indications of a craving for an authoritative type of doctrinal teaching. It is not accidental that both Roman and fundamentalist teachings appeal to many people today. Living in a world that lacks any common religion or philosophy, and in which conflicting ideologies struggle for mastery, it is not surprising if many long for a dictated belief. One of the experiences which sometimes alarms those of us who have been speaking about Christian truth to generations of students is the discovery of the way in which many of them now want to be told what to believe. We need to think carefully about our reaction to this situation. If we are not prepared to coerce men and women, at least we ought to be leading them; if we are apprehensive of their demand for 'authoritative' teaching, we cannot be content that they should receive instruction that carries no authority.

(b) The theological questions which are asked are themselves highly significant. Firstly, they tend to be based upon ways of thinking, both theological and scientific, which belong to a previous generation. It is platitudinous to say that the pew is a generation behind the pulpit, but whose fault is that? The complexity and fluidity of theological scholarship have, I think, led to something approaching despair about the difficulty of interpreting doctrine to the masses. Those who believe that, out of a period of critical study of the Bible in which at first destructive results seemed strongest, positive results of great value to Christian living have emerged, and those who believe that amid the conflicts that characterize the contemporary revival of theological study the meaning of the gospel is being made plainer, must recognize that we tend to be less successful in communicating doctrine than were our predecessors, whether they lived in periods of conservative quietude or of theological upheaval. Yet we serve a community in which general education is more advanced than ever before.

Secondly, the theological questions that are commonly asked show that the true relation between doctrine and life has been obscured. In an American journal, a year or two ago, a girl was reported as saying: 'The ministers insist on talking about social matters, like dating and drinking, though the young people want to study comparative religion, original sin and really important subjects like that.' This is a revealing remark which merits attention. It illustrates the theological curiosity about which I have previously spoken, but it also shows how 'really important' theological questions are assumed to be remote from the details of moral behaviour and from social problems. We should be foolish to blame the girl, even if she was yielding to the temptation to escape from personal decision into the pleasures of intellectual debate. Rather must we see in her attitude a reflection of the teaching to which she had listened, teaching which was ethical without being doctrinal, and in which a limited number of individual moral problems was isolated from the totality of personal and social moral responsibility. What this girl was unconsciously seeking was a worthy pastoral theology.

(c) Finally, the confused scene at which we have glanced reminds us that a Church in which Christian doctrine has lost much of its pastoral content is set in a world which is fast abandoning belief in God. Will the third generation of children outside the Church's influence ask the kind of theological questions which most children have previously asked? I doubt it. If our parents, grandparents and their parents had had little or no interest in medical knowledge and in medical healing, should we be very interested in these matters? If theology is thought of as a specialized study, pursued by students, or by a class of 'religious' people whose religion is a form of escape from the common world of affairs, it is little wonder that for an increasing number of people it appears to have no importance. The contemporary lack of pastoral theology is, I believe, one important contributory factor in the godlessness of today; its revival is one part of the Church's evangelical duty.

Throughout this discussion it has become clear that some ways of thinking about Christian theology minimize, or even destroy, its pastoral character, and that some ways of thinking about Christian life minimize the place of theology in the cure of souls. In the remainder of this chapter we shall be considering these misunderstandings. I shall approach each of them from the point of view of that somewhat fictitious composite figure, 'the man in the pew'. I do this because the theme of this book requires us to ask what Christian doctrine means to him, and not merely what it means to the scholar, but we shall see that behind popular misunderstandings lie tendencies within academic theology itself. In the next few pages we shall be approaching somewhat technical theological discussion, but always (I hope) with the needs of the 'common man' in mind.

II. THE FUNCTION OF THEOLOGICAL STATEMENTS

The first popular notion to which we turn is the belief that formal statements of a theological character, both in the historic Creeds themselves and in theological pronouncements of all types, have, at best, very limited functions. Whilst few Christians imagine that Christian doctrine is entirely unconnected with Christian living, and whilst there is some fresh awareness of the place of theology in preaching, it is widely held that theology only concerns what is described as 'the intellect', and that since most people are not 'intellectual', doctrine can matter little to them.

I believe that this attitude has been encouraged by two tendencies in scholarly theology. The reader is asked to remember (in this section and in the following sections) that I am not suggesting that all scholars who hold the views mentioned themselves draw the conclusions to which I shall refer; I am seeking to point out conclusions which *may* be drawn. Nor is it to be inferred that the ideas and attitudes which call for discussion are necessarily erroneous; I myself believe many of them to be of value. But in theology, as in all other human activities, that which is good often has unfortunate by-products of which we need to be aware. The two matters first to be discussed are: (1) the purpose of the Creeds, and (2) the nature of theological statements in general.

(1) Ever since Harnack, it has been popular to think of the historic Creeds as representing a degeneration from the simplicities of the gospel. Long after that belief has faded from serious theological scholarship, its legacy has remained in the life of the Churches. In particular, the opinion lingers that the only function of the Creeds was a negative one; even speakers and writers who should be better informed, assert that the sole purpose of the Creeds was the exclusion of heresy.

Even if that assumption were true, the pastoral significance of the historic Creeds would be considerable. It is indeed true that part of the purpose of those who formulated them was the exclusion of heresy; but for what reason? It was not because ambitious and learned clerics wished to triumph over their intellectual adversaries, even if sometimes such motives corrupted good men; nor was it because the well-being of the clever few was at stake. When the Church of the first four centuries wrestled to describe the Person of Christ or the doctrine of the Trinity, it was, it is true, putting up fences or warning-notices. But it was giving warning of ways of thinking about God and about Jesus which would—if followed—lead unlettered men and scholars alike away from the saving truth, away from that knowledge of God and of Him whom He has sent which is eternal life (Jn 17[3]). Not the least of the pastoral duties of the church is this protection against heresy.

But, in point of fact, the origin of Creeds is found in several purposes which were very positive. Recent work by many scholars has made this fact much plainer. The best brief introduction to this subject is provided by Oscar Cullman in *The Earliest Christian Confessions*; fuller treatment is given by J. N. D. Kelly in *Early Christian Creeds*.

These and other scholars have drawn our attention to the fragmentary, yet formal statements in the New Testament itself. These range from what was probably the earliest, and certainly the shortest confession: JESUS IS LORD to formulae such as JESUS IS THE CHRIST or JESUS IS THE SON OF GOD and to binitarian and trinitarian confessions, that is, affirmations about the Father and the Son and about Father, Son and Spirit. From a careful study of this scriptural evidence and of other Christian writings in the first three centuries, Cullmann arrives (p. 18) at the following 'five simultaneous causes' for the construction and use of Confessions of Faith:

(i) Baptism and Catechumenism
(ii) Regular worship (liturgy and preaching)
(iii) Exorcism
(iv) Persecution
(v) Polemic against heresies

Before commenting upon the significance of this list for our present inquiry, I must make reference to a modification of it made by J. N. D. Kelly.

Kelly questions the now common assertion that the first function of declaratory creeds was their use in baptism. In a closely documented argument, which cannot be summarized here, he contends that Creeds played no part in baptism before the fourth century, and that even then their rôle in baptism was only secondary. It seems necessary to mention this divergence of view, if only not to deceive any reader who may be unfamiliar with the relevant literature. But if Kelly modifies one item in Cullmann's list, he does so only greatly to strengthen another item, namely, the role of creedal confessions in *catechetical teaching*. About this he has much to say which is of great importance for the understanding of the way in which the Church grew. He sums up by saying: 'Declaratory Creeds may therefore be regarded as a by-product of the Church's fully-developed catechetical system', and he shows that his negative conclusions about their early use in baptism is not, after all, of first importance. If, as seems probable, doctrinal affirmations belonged for a long time to preparation for, rather than to the actual rite of baptism, it was nevertheless to that event that the catechist looked forward. 'The catechetical instruction of which the declaratory creeds were convenient summaries was instruction *with a view to baptism* . . . So closely did [this] instruction dovetail into the ceremony of initiation . . . that the single word baptism . . . could be used to cover them both . . .'[1]

This long reference to Kelly's book reinforces what has already been said about the catechetical instruction of the early church. If the scheme given on page 15 is examined again, it will readily be seen that declaratory Creeds would most fittingly summarize the teaching given under (1); their relevance to all the other items in this scheme of instruction is a matter about which more will be said as this book progresses. This catechetical use of Confessions of Faith is both a rebuttal of the opinion that Creeds developed purely in opposition to heresy, and also another reminder that pastoral theology is part of the equipment necessary for evangelism. It is perhaps worth adding that the practice of infant baptism places upon us a special duty in this respect. Whilst scholars sort out the 'theology of initiation', the work of the Church must go on, and those whose baptism preceeds instruction are in no less need of theological training than those who are baptised as believers.

We must now return to Cullmann's list of the 'simultaneous causes' of precise theological statements or formulae. Only the last item in this list refers to their function in relation to heresy; all the others concern the daily life of Christians. In addition to their catechetical use already discussed, such statements had their place in the Church's regular worship. Can it be doubted that worship which excludes repetition of either the historic Creeds or of Confessions of Faith in scriptural terms is impoverished worship? The Church's Faith may be, and happily often is, expressed in hymns and prayers and sermons, but must these take the place of more formal statements?

Cullmann's reference to exorcism raises questions about the existence and nature of evil spirits into which we cannot enter here, but even if we prefer to speak (in a not very clear, 'demythologizing' sense) about 'demonic forces', is there not still place for confession of the beliefs which both recognize and pronounce sentence upon all evil powers?

Finally, if any aspect of the early Church's use of doctrinal Confessions has special point for us today, it is the use of them to fortify believers in time of persecution. It is significant that the faithful Christians in Nazi Germany came to be known as 'the Confessional Church'; one bugle that sounded the defeat of that

[1] J. N. D. Kelly, *Early Christian Creeds*, p. 51.

tyranny was the dogmatic assertion of the Christian Faith. Perhaps only those who have said 'I BELIEVE' in a concentration camp, or with secret police in the congregation, know what Creeds are really for! But the repetition of Creeds without the help that is provided by theological instruction is as injurious to Christians as is the absence of firm and clear beliefs. Evil, whether human or of any other kind, cannot be conquered by an incantation; the lives of Christians cannot be sustained by mere words.

I have devoted space to this subject, although the evidence is easily accessible to students, because I believe that every Church member needs to recognize the place that definite doctrinal affirmation had in the Church of early years and the place that it needs to occupy to-day.[2]

(2) The fear that all theological words are 'mere words', having no reference to any non-verbal reality, is the second of the two points of view which fall for discussion in this section. Here again, scholarly points of view lie behind popular notions, and in this instance these points of view are both theological and philosophical.

Much recent theological discussion has centred upon the nature of divine revelation. The remark, first made (I believe) by William Temple, 'Revelation is not in propositions [statements], but in events', has become a cliché in much contemporary theology. This assertion usefully points attention to those events of sacred history, recorded in the Bible, which Christians believe to be the supreme revelatory work of God; but this attempt to limit the meaning of revelation to the 'events' themselves is theologically unsatisfactory and religiously unhelpful. In the end, I believe, this well-intended effort to liberate Christian faith from its relation to theological statements makes any intelligible account of revelation impossible.

That Jesus died under Pontius Pilate is not a theological statement; that Jesus died for our sins is; it is the latter alone which is

[2] After this book had been completed I received a copy of *The Faith of the Church*, a statement issued by a Joint Commission on Church Union set up by the Congrational Union of Australia and New Zealand and the Methodist and Presbyterian Churches of Australia. In this exceptionally lucid report the matters dealt with in the above section of this chapter are discussed in detail, with ample citation from the scholars to whom I have referred. The 'Rule of Faith', which existed long before the earliest formularies that preceded the Apostles' and so-called Nicene Creeds, and the Confessions of the Reformation are fully discussed and the relevance of all these matters to the contemporary Church is set forth. In so far as this document represents the Conviction of these Churches toward Creeds, we have evidence of an attitude which is bound greatly to influence the pastoral theology of these denominations of Christ's Church in Australia.

gospel. That after Pentecost the disciples behaved quite differently from before, and that the Church then began to take shape are historical statements; that these events happened through the operation of the Holy Spirit is a theological statement. Events without meaning can have no revelatory content, and as soon as we consider meaning we require statements—in this instance theological statements.

The theologian is tempted to hope that he can evade the criticisms of many contemporary philosophers by releasing Christian belief from theological language. But the challenge which the analytical philosophers offer must be met, not escaped; it would be a worthless kind of Christian defence which silenced the critical philosophers at the cost of abandoning the doctrine which the Church exists to teach.

I believe that, in all branches of theological study, increasing attention needs to be paid to the dominant school of British philosophy. As I understand this type of philosophy, it has now passed beyond its earlier stage, in which all statements not verifiable by sense-experience were treated as either tautologies or mere expressions of emotion. This philosophical attitude was merely old-fashioned materialism wearing a new dress. The linguistic analysts now recognize that different words have different kinds of meaning, because they serve diverse purposes; they ask—and rightly ask—what is the purpose of theological language? If some philosophers express doubt about the possibility of any satisfactory answer being found to this query, and profess a somewhat unfamiliar kind of wistful agnosticism, others look more hopefully for an answer.

The influence of this approach to language, and to theological words in particular, extends far beyond academic circles. The man in the sitting-room is listening to broadcasts by philosophers and by other able men and women who share their views. In senior classes of schools and in universities questions derived from these sources are already being asked; it will be surprising if they do not soon begin to be asked (in somewhat different form) by a wider public. How can statements about God mean anything? *What* do they mean? Such questions are not as new as some of the questioners appear to imagine; Aquinas would be at home with most of them. Whether or not his teaching about analogical language provides part of the answer to modern questions about the meaning of theological statements, it is part of the Church's responsibility to seek and provide an answer. We need many Christian students, trained in the necessary disciplines, who will engage in conversation with contemporary philosophers. Whoever he be who asks, 'What do you mean when you say *that* about God?'—whether he be a university teacher or a youngster in an open-air speaker's crowd—he deserves a respectful and an intelligible answer. This, too, is part of the function of pastoral theology.

Only one comment can be made here upon the kind of answer that needs to be given to this inquiry about the meaning of theological statements. Theological language began to be spoken and developed within believing communities. That is true about the theology of all religions; it is most patently true about Christian theology. Although most words in the Christian vocabulary came from outside the life of the Church, they were employed in order to describe and interpret that life.

Christian theological language is *for* Christian living; in no other context has it meaning. Hence, nobody can hope to learn this language in a meaningful way if he is entirely out of touch with those who know that they need this language, and who know why they need it. It is only within the experience of God's relationship with men that doctrinal words have significance. We should not expect to understand the terminology of botanists without reference to plant life, nor of sociologists apart from awareness of human beings. The Bible itself is a largely unintelligible book, and certainly an easily misunderstood one, if it is not read within a living Church. Christian theology, whether in the Bible or elsewhere, only becomes luminous within the cure of souls; to that extent *all* theology is pastoral theology.

III. SOME ATTEMPTS TO DIVORCE THEOLOGY AND EXPERIENCE

Religious language can only have meaning in relation to religious experience; that is one of the conclusions to which this chapter has so far led. Does not this imply that experience, rather than theology, is the pastor's field of study, and that experience, rather than doctrine, is the need of those who are shepherds?

No Christian denomination lays more emphasis upon 'experience' than does Methodism. The early Methodist custom of encouraging recent converts and mature believers to 'give their testimonies' is by no means obsolete; candidates for the Ministry are still required repeatedly to recount their 'experience'. Methodism has been described, perhaps more graphically than illuminatingly, as possessing a 'theology of the warmed heart'. Even a discussion of the significance of experience may appear to some readers to border on treason, when it is undertaken by a Methodist. Yet if pastoral experience has taught me anything at all, it has shown the misunderstandings that gather around this perfectly proper emphasis upon personal Christian experience.

Once again we look first at these misunderstandings in their popular expressions. 'It's not what we believe, but what we experience that matters', 'It's not knowing about God, but knowing God', 'It's not what the Church teaches, but what *I* know'—such are some of the half-truths which in practice become hindrances to the truth. The effects of this way of thinking become quickly apparent to the pastor who listens to those to whom he speaks. He finds people seeking for an 'experience' rather than for God; he discovers them waiting (with much or little hope) that somehow their emotions will be stirred; he learns that some who have long been practising Christians know virtually nothing about the doctrines of the Church and, in many instances, little about the teaching of the Bible. He even finds, as I have already hinted, that curiosity about theological matters, which is not hard to quicken in most adults and which is almost instinctive in children, has become dulled in many adults within the Church. Some Christians even fear that theology must inevitably injure experience; many imagine that religious experience renders needless any attention to Christian doctrine.

There is sufficient truth mixed with these erroneous views to invite us to tread warily in criticizing them. It might be argued that there is strong support for them, both in (1) the type of philosophy known as *Existentialist* and (2) the kind of theology which is described as *Encounter* or *I-Thou* theology. As one who is very much indebted to many exponents of these ideas, I wish to suggest ways in which they may be mishandled.

(1) The term 'existential' shares with 'eschatalogical' the dubious privilege of being used as a cover for many ideas and much confused thought. It should never be forgotten that, were we to count heads, there are probably more atheistic than theistic existentialists. When the existentialist position is taken by a Christian, I take it to involve the assertion that God can only be

known in the actual, concrete existence of venturing faith. As such it is an important, although not very original observation. But when the further opinion is held that personal decision removes the need for doctrine, and renders superfluous all enquiry about historical truth and about the meaning of theological statements, existentialism becomes a snare. It very easily leads to the assumption that what we believe *about* God has little relevance to belief *in* Him. Christian doctrine then becomes, at best, a somewhat unnecessary way of talking about experience, and, at worst, a hindrance to Christian life.

All the many forms of contemporary existentialism are the heirs (often somewhat illegitimate) of Kierkegaard. But as Hermann Diem has recently reminded us, Kierkegaard himself never made the divorce between doctrine and experience which many of his followers have made, and which has led them in such diverse directions. Kierkegaard, as Diem shows, was content to presuppose the truth of the Christian revelation and of Church dogmatics. He himself wrote: 'Doctrine, as usually expounded, is on the whole correct. I am not disputing about that. My sole concern is how far it can be effective.' He felt, Diem comments, that his sole work was to show how one becomes a Christian. 'He proposed to be merely a corrective to existing Christianity, merely a touch of cinnamon to the food of normal Christian doctrine.'[3]

Kierkegaard was engaged upon pastoral theology. Whether his method is one that should be copied is debatable; it is certain that the attempt to combine his method with indifference to the doctrinal theology upon which his work was a commentary is disastrous. It is one matter to talk about what it means to have faith in a God about whom much is believed; it is quite a different matter to make 'knowing God' an alternative to 'knowing about' Him, or 'decision for faith' an escape from the need to learn the facts without which Christian faith is impossible.

The type of 'existentialism' which I have in mind recalls the frequent misuse of John 7^{17}: 'If any man's will is to do his will he shall know whether the teaching is from God or whether I am speaking on my own authority.' One has often heard these words cited as a proof of the superiority of doing to believing, of 'practical Christianity' to Christian belief. In fact, of course, the meaning is

[3] H. Diem, *Dogmatics* (Eng. trans.), p. 20. Much in this important book is of importance to the advanced student of theology in general and of pastoral theology in particular.

very different. It is only those who want to do God's will rather than their own who will be able to recognize the divine authority in the teaching of Jesus; it is our attitude towards Christ's doctrine that is the point at issue, not the relative insignificance of that doctrine.

The commonly made contrast between 'knowing' and 'knowing about' is by no means a clear one. It is true that I may know much about X without having met him; in that sense I know about him without knowing him in the way that I know Y, whom I have met. I cannot know (meet) Y without learning something about him, but if I know very little about him, I may (in another sense) 'know' X better than I know Y.

The parallel with man's knowledge of God is not complete; we cannot 'know' God by sense-experience—'No man has seen God at any time'. Leaving aside for the moment questions about mystical experience and communion with God, it must be emphasized that it is impossible to claim that any man can 'know' the God and Father of our Lord Jesus Christ unless he 'knows about' Him. It is, indeed, true that when we learn about Him we discover how greatly we were indebted to Him before we recognized our debt.

> ... every virtue we possess,
> And every conquest won,
> And every thought of holiness,
> Are His alone.

But God remains anonymous until we learn about Him, and it was precisely because an anonymous God would not suffice that God 'chose the Jews', and sent His Son, and gave the Holy Spirit and commissioned His Church to speak about Him.

In so far as 'existentialist' philosophy speaks to us about personal decision and about the response which must be made by the whole personality, it is to be welcomed; when it invites us to despise the intellectual element in our response to God, it is mischievous. It is then, indeed, self-contradictory, for existentialism is itself a philosophical position, and a difficult one at that.

(2) The type of theological approach to which we now turn has much in common with existentialism. *Encounter-theology* is the doctrine that man only knows God as God 'meets' him, as he is confronted by God. An alternative name for this type of theology is *I-Thou theology*, which affirms that God is not an Object to be examined by us, but a Subject who addresses us.

Buber's famous book on this theme has had many varied successors from other pens. Once again there is great value in these ways of expressing truths that have long been familiar to Christians. The Bible is a book not about man's way to God, but about God's way to man; Christian life cannot be lived in the same way as a man reads the map of a foreign country in his study, but only as a traveller follows the map on a long journey. Yet 'the map' is not irrelevant. God does 'encounter' us, but this does not mean that we do not need to learn where and how this encounter takes place.

It is to be feared that teaching of this type is often fallaciously simple. Only by the swift use of apparently easy metaphor does it seem to by-pass old and troublesome questions, such as those about the inspiration of biblical writers, the Incarnation, the work of the Holy Spirit and the interpretative work of the Church. These strictly theological questions can only be avoided if it is assumed that some way to the saving knowledge of God is discoverable which makes them irrelevant. If there were such a way, the long history of Israel, the Birth, Life, Death and Resurrection of Christ, the gift of the Holy Spirit and the creation of the Church would become needless superfluities, or merely complicated additions to the essentials of faith. That is a position which Christians who write theology about 'encounter' can hardly wish to reach.

So we return, from this brief reference to scholarly theology, to the common man's point of view. When he says that we must know God rather than know about Him, what does he mean? Does he mean that all Christian life must be based upon mystical experience, in the sense of direct, unmediated awareness of God? Perhaps some do mean precisely this.

If mystical experience is made the necessary foundation of Christian life, several questions need to be asked. Has such experience ever been enjoyed by more than a few men and women? Have Christian mystics themselves ever suggested that their own experience was continuous, or pointed to it as the *supreme* evidence for belief in God? Mystical experience, by its very character, is incommunicable (it is of 'things that cannot be uttered'); is it not true that when a mystic speaks about God he does so in whatever theological vocabulary is familiar to him? If mystical experience is the essential, we must admit that few can be Christians, and that these few can never be evangelists.

THEOLOGY AND THE CURE OF SOULS

I do not wish to minimize the import of the 'glimpses of His presence' which God, in His goodness, allows to many who are by no means possessed of mystical gifts. Perhaps He grants these to us because we are not strong enough to live without them? But 'Blessed are those who have not seen, and yet believe' (Jn 20[29]). And even for those who have 'seen' it is still true, as A. Raymond George has demonstrated in *Communion with God in the New Testament*, that direct vision of God belongs to heaven, not to earth. It is not enough for us to assert that Christ is the *only* Mediator; we must take seriously the fact that He *is* the Mediator. If we take that fact seriously, the necessity for the Bible and the Church, which witness to Christ, becomes plain, and the place of doctrine about God, and of pastoral theology which deals with that doctrine, becomes clearly apparent.

Perhaps one of the most popular meanings given to 'experience' (viewed as an alternative to doctrinal belief) is that of emotional experience. This is the notion, previously mentioned, that religion belongs to the 'heart' rather than to the 'head', and in the Christian circles with which I am most familiar this is the most common misunderstanding. Even the collapse of an outmoded 'faculty' psychology (which treated mind, emotion and will as separate 'parts' of man) has not shaken this view. So powerful is it, that it is read into the biblical references to 'heart', although it is quite clear that neither Old nor New Testament writers intended (by words thus translated) to refer particularly to the emotions; 'heart', in the Bible, always refers to the whole inner life of man, often with special emphasis upon that aspect of his nature which we call reason.

Of course, emotion is of the utmost importance; in Christian living, as in all human activity, it is the supreme driving force. If the sum of God's commandments is to love God and our neighbour, emotion can hardly be excluded, even though love is more than an emotion. But untold harm has been done by this contrast between emotion and thought. If the gospel is believed, it must by its very nature stir us in the emotional depths of our being, but to enjoy our emotions is no necessary part of, and may well be a hindrance to, the total response of thought, emotion and will to God. How perverse have been many of the references to Wesley's 'warmed heart', and how many Methodists know about the warmed heart without knowing why it was warm! It was as

Wesley listened to the reading of a very 'intellectual' preface to a theological commentary upon the most doctrinal of all the Epistles that he came to a sure and certain trust that Christ died for *his* sins. Wesley did not travel the country preaching about his emotions; he preached and taught in language which many of his present-day followers would deem impossibly 'theological'.

If these comments appear to be severe, that severity is due to a conviction that all attempts to found Christian life upon feelings is destructive of that life, and, especially, of the profound emotional quality of deep faith in God. I have mentioned one way in which this mistake is sometimes made by Methodists, because I have no right to speak of other Christian communions; perhaps others will recognize ways in which aesthetic feelings, kindled by beauty in ritual, music and other artistic creation, can become a substitute for, instead of an expression of, Christian belief and Christian faith. D. Martyn Lloyd-Jones (who is respected as one of the leaders of conservative evangelical thought in Great Britain) has wisely written:

.... in presenting the Christian gospel we must never, in the first place, make a *direct* approach to the emotions or to the will. The emotions and the will should always be influenced through the mind. Truth is intended to come to the *mind*. The normal course is for the emotions and the will to be affected by the truth after it has entered and gripped the mind. It seems to me that this is a principle of Holy Scripture.[4]

IV. THE INTERDEPENDENCE OF THEOLOGY AND EXPERIENCE

We have noticed some of the ways in which the rôle of theology is minimized, and in which doctrinal belief is separated from the essential nature of Christian living. What, then, is the true relationship between theology and experience?

It is difficult to provide a concise answer to this question, because both 'theology' and 'experience' are portmanteau words covering many meanings. Obviously, some types of theological study must be reserved to the specialists; equally clearly, there is a vast difference between the possession of theological information and opinions and commitment to Christian discipleship. (About the different kinds of 'theology' something will be said in Chapter 12.) There is also a gulf between those who rest upon experience which is individual and those who contrast theology with the corporate

[4] *Conversions, Psychological and Spiritual*, p. 39.

experience of Christendom. To substitute 'my experience' for learning from the Bible and from the Church is a form of egoism which loses none of its viciousness because it is camouflaged with an appearance of piety. To say (as I must), 'My faith must be *my* faith' should not imply that I consider myself to have won and kept my faith by myself alone.

It may be asked, however, whether, in the wider, corporate sense of 'experience', we should not say that experience is always prior to doctrine. I think not. The point of view which I hope to illustrate as this book proceeds is that doctrine and experience, experience and theological interpretation, are interdependent.

An American writer on pastoral matters, Carroll A. Wise, has expressed the opposite view to mine: 'Religious experience produces the interpretation; the interpretation never produces the experience.' Commenting upon this remark, D. D. Evans has written:

> Wise tends to depreciate the dynamic role of traditional Christian concepts in creating religious insight. He rightly emphasises the importance of individual human experience.... But, compared with traditional theology, he minimises the creative power of the Christian interpretation, the word of God, in shaping the individual's experience. . . . In religious thinking (as in other thinking), there is an intimate interdependence between experience and interpretative framework.[5]

I do not think that Evans's comment requires amplification so far as it concerns the experience of the individual. It seems manifestly false to say that *his* experience always produces interpretation and is never produced by it; if that were so, what would be the point of reading the Bible or listening to sermons? We must, however, press this interdependence of theology and experience much further. In so doing we approach many major theological questions, such as the relationship between Church and Bible, the place of tradition in Christian belief, and the 'authority' of preaching—questions far beyond the scope of this book.

This only can be said here: at every stage in the revelatory work of God (as Christians understand it) interpretation and experience, doctrine and both individual and corporate experience, have been bound up with each other. The Old Testament is the record both of the experience of Israel and of the teaching in Israel; it was

---

[5] Donald D. Evans, 'Pastoral Counselling and Traditional Theology (*Scottish Journal of Theology*, June 1958). Evans cites the above quotation (and similar ones) from Carroll A. Wise, *Pastoral Counselling, Its Theory and Practice*.

through what they experienced that the Hebrews learnt about God, and it was through what they learnt about God that they entered into new experiences. So it was with the Christian Church from the beginning; so it is now with the Church, when it is a living Church.

It is when we consider Jesus Himself, however, that the point that I am trying to make becomes most clear. If ever the word 'encounter' is an appropriate word, it is in reference to His encounter with men, both in the days of His flesh and through the Holy Spirit since. But teaching (and theological teaching at that) is an essential aspect of that encounter. It is sometimes said that there is 'no theology in the teaching of Jesus'; this somewhat absurd statement merely illustrates the popular misuse of the term 'theology' to describe what is obscure, abstract, unintelligible. Only if the Kingdom of God is misunderstood in terms of a social order waiting to be 'built' from an ethical blue-print provided in the Gospels, only if the profoundly theological statements and implications of the sayings and parables of Jesus are ignored, only if all that He is reported (even by the earliest records) as having said about Himself and His Father is brushed aside, only if, in short, an imaginary picture of the teaching of Jesus replaces the only picture that we possess, can the illusion be maintained that theological doctrine did not play a decisive part in the impact that Christ made upon men and in the experience resulting therefrom. Even the enemies of Jesus knew better than this, and when they accused Him of blasphemous teaching, they were, in this respect, nearer to understanding Him than some of His subsequent admirers have been.

In recent study of the New Testament a clarification of our understanding of the Gospels has emerged from what at first appeared to many to be wholly destructive criticism. One thing that has been made plain is that in the Gospels we have the Church's testimony to Jesus, and the result is that we can begin to understand better why certain sayings and actions of the Lord were written down and others were omitted. In particular we can partially trace the *pastoral* motive that guided this selection. It would be rewarding to follow that line of thought in detail, but it is one that calls for all the skills of New Testament scholarship and the task lies outside the scope of this present book. Even the inexpert reader, however, can apply the principle in a general way, and he will find that much in the Gospels becomes meaningful if he attempts to imagine why this word of the Master's, this action of His, was recounted by the first Christians and written down by the evangelists.

One small illustration must suffice. J. C. O'Neill has recently made a careful examination of the six *Amen* sayings in Luke—the sayings prefaced by 'the only foreign word' in Luke or Acts, a word which draws special attention to the quoted words of Jesus. He shows that these sayings bind together God's plan of salvation in history with the call to a Christian life. These are words about the daily life of Christians, the life of those who have already received the promises of Christ, who can face death in peace, and who know that, at the End Jesus will welcome them into His Kingdom. 'Thus', says O'Neill—

> the Amen sayings are a guide to ordinary Christians, produced when it became clear that they would live and die without seeing the end of history or the coming of the Kingdom. We are witnessing the *beginning of Pastoral Theology*: its 'faithful sayings' selected from the words of the Lord himself.[6]

'Experience' is, we have repeatedly seen, an ambiguous word. As a reminder that Christian faith is more than coldly intellectual assent to statements about God, as a pointer to the nature of faith as sure trust in God through His Son by the power of the Holy Spirit, and as a term to describe Christian thinking, feeling and doing in its entirety, 'experience' is a helpful term. But if it turns our attention away from the need to learn about God and to consider what belief in Him involves, if it makes us impatient with the questions that men ask about God or with the statements about God made by Christ and by his disciples, or if it bids us hope that we can know God for ourselves in some way that is wholly private, then it becomes a dangerous word. Only as we learn that the theology of the Christian Church is itself part of the experience of the Church, can we discover both the limitations in all theology and the necessity for theology; only as we discover what theology can do within the cure of souls, can we rightly recognize what it can never do. Theology itself may be a form of idolatry; indeed, all idolatry is a kind of theology, and only a theology which is part of the worship of the true God can cast out theology that is idolatrous. But to abandon theology itself is to abandon part of

[6] *Journal of Theological Studies*, April 1959, p. 9. Italics mine.

our worship of God, and to think that the common people do not need theology is to despise both God and them.

We have now completed our introductory study of the cure of souls and of the place of theology in that ministry, and we have considered some of the reasons for the decline of interest in pastoral theology. Throughout the preceding chapters instances have been given of the relationship between Christian doctrine and Christian life; it has been argued that the relationship between theology and Christian experience is that of interdependence.

The two following parts of this book contain illustrations of that interdependence. For convenience, in Part Two I offer examples of ways in which particular Christian doctrines have direct pastoral relevance, and in Part Three I seek to show how specific human needs call for the understanding and exposition of specific Christian beliefs. In each chapter suggestions will also be made about diverse characteristics of the purpose and methods of pastoral theology.

Like all attempts to divide the indivisible, this division of subject matter could easily lead us astray. Each of the particular doctrines referred to in one place could equally well have been mentioned in several other contexts, for Christian belief is characterized by wholeness. Every theological teacher knows that almost any theological question is relevant to any subject that he is discussing, and that no one doctrine can be fully interpreted save by the light of the whole body of doctrine. I do not wish to suggest that human need A must always be met by doctrine B, and so on. The pastor needs to have a mind stored with as much of the wealth of Christian truth as he can receive; how much theology, in the more technical sense of the word, each believer requires is one of the important questions with which pastoral theology must be greatly concerned, and about which a little more will be said later. It may, however, be confidently asserted that the specialist in pastoral care needs to be watchful lest he become exclusively interested in some particular doctrines, and behave in the things of the spirit like a physician whose preoccupation with the study of rheumatic conditions leads him to diagnose every pain as a case of rheumatism. It may well be that personal interest has tended to guide my own selection of illustrative doctrines, but I have attempted to choose those which have special significance for pastoral work today.

PART TWO

FROM DOCTRINE TO PASTORAL CARE

CHAPTER FOUR

THE DOCTRINE OF THE TRINITY AND THE CURE OF SOULS

BEFORE the main theme of this chapter is introduced, a word of warning must be given about our whole approach to the study of pastoral theology. We need to beware that we do not decide theological questions by a test that is purely pragmatic; we must beware of the peril of seeking to determine the truth of a belief by its ability to produce beneficial results.

It has often been said that a theology that cannot be preached cannot be true theology, but that does not mean that everything that can be said from a pulpit is true theology; similarly, it may rightly be said that a theology that cannot be applied pastorally is immediately suspect, but it does not follow that every belief which has beneficial results is true belief. The grounds for Christian belief are not established by this kind of test. It is not my purpose to discuss the grounds of Christian belief, but the reader may care to relieve any tedium involved in reading these pages by seeking to discover points at which I have unwittingly distorted Christian truth to serve my case.

It is necessary, however, to be equally on guard against the paralysing effects of a fear of wishful-thinking. At the present time, for various reasons, we are specially prone to this fear; it is significant that the word 'propaganda', which was once a term that signified the spreading of truth—as in the title, 'Society for the Propagation of the Gospel', now suggests the attempt to establish a desired result by the use of lies. Yet the fact that I am hungry has no bearing upon the actuality of the food on the table, though it may have a great deal to do with the energy with which I prepare the meal and the manner in which I eat it; and similarly, the facts about God are in no way determined by my wishes or lack of wishes; He is no less and no more real because I want Him to be so. But He cannot be to me what He would be, unless I 'hunger and thirst' for Him. It is as foolish to despise the usefulness of theology as it is to make utility the basis of theological conviction.

I. THE TRIUNE GOD

We begin our study of illustrations of ways in which Christian theological study must be directed to pastoral needs by considering the doctrine of the tri-unity of God. This is our starting-point, because this doctrine, which is the climax of Christian belief, is the doctrine which is of supreme importance for Christian living.

I understand that many students of theology were surprised that Karl Barth opened his massive *Church Dogmatics* with a prolonged discussion of the doctrine of the Trinity. (This theme occupies the second chapter of the Prolegomena, the first volume of this many-volumed work.) But where else can a theologian begin, if he is about to write, not a work of speculative or philosophical theology, but (as Barth describes his purpose) a study of dogmatics as 'the self-test to which the Christian Church puts herself in respect of the content' of her peculiar language about God'? He must begin where the Bible ends, with the developed faith of the Church. But in starting with the doctrine of the Trinity, Barth begins with the end that was arrived at in the Bible itself, not with what first began to be believed after the Bible had been completed.

The oft-repeated statement: 'There is no doctrine of the Trinity in the New Testament', is one of those ambiguous remarks which have, by constant reiteration, led to grave misunderstanding, and which have encouraged the divorce of theology from Christian life and from the pastoral ministry. When it is claimed, even by serious students, that the New Testament contains no trinitarian doctrine, it must be assumed that what is being referred to is the formulation of that doctrine in the Creeds, especially in the Athanasian; but the statement then becomes a mere glimpse of the obvious. If it be asserted that the New Testament held *no* triune doctrine, and that the Christians of whom these writings speak did not worship the triune God, then the truth of such an assertion must be strenuously denied.

Confusion about this matter has been largely due to two related failures: the failure to recognize the multiplicity of New Testament references to Father, Son and Spirit, and the failure to correct the false assumption that Paul wholly identified the Son and the Spirit. The latter error has been exposed by so many scholars, who have shown it to be mainly based upon an almost

THE DOCTRINE OF THE TRINITY

certainly incorrect interpretation of one text (2 Cor 3^{17}), that space need not be devoted to this subject.[1] But the existence of a trinitarian pattern (or structure) in the New Testament requires brief consideration.

In *Early Christian Creeds* (Chapter I), J. N. D. Kelly has clearly demonstrated the existence of a 'host of passages' which reveal this trinitarian pattern. There are, of course, a great many other passages which reveal a binitarian outlook, that is to say, which refer exclusively to Father and Son, and little imagination is required to see why this twofold way of thinking should have been (as Kelly puts it) 'deeply impressed upon the thought of primitive Christianity'. But (Kelly adds) it appears that the trinitarian schema was 'no less deeply impressed'.

The notion that the only references to the Trinity are to be found in the grace (2 Cor 13^{14}) and in the baptismal command (Mt 28^{19}) is extraordinarily widespread and completely mistaken. Among the many significant references given by Kelly, the reader, if he is not familiar with the evidence, may care to note 1 Corinthians 2^{10-16}, $6^{11, 13ff}$, 12^3; 2 Corinthians 1^{21f}, 3^3; Galatians 3^{11-14}; and Colossians 1^{6-8}. But there are very many more passages which reveal, not a fixity of wording, nor a Creed of the later type, but what Kelly has called 'a trinitarian ground-plan'. Any reader who studies this matter will come to share Kelly's impression that

the conception of the threefold manifestation of the Godhead was embedded deeply in Christian thinking from the start, and provided a ready-to-hand mould in which the ideas of the apostolic writers took shape. If Trinitarian creeds are rare, the Trinitarian pattern which was to dominate all later creeds was already part and parcel of the Christian tradition of doctrine (p. 23).

This truth has been admirably summarized by another distinguished expert, H. E. W. Turner, who remarks that Christians '*lived trinitarianly*' long before the construction of Nicene orthodoxy.[2]

The Epistle to the Ephesians is especially full of these trinitarian references,[3] one example of which must suffice. In Chapter 2^{11ff}, the writer is describing the unity of Gentiles with Jews in the

---

[1] See G. S. Hendry, *The Holy Spirit in Christian Theology*, Chapter I.
[2] H. E. W. Turner, *The Pattern of Christian Truth*.
[3] Ch. 1^3, $^{11-13, 17}$, 2^{18-22}, $3^{3-7, 14-17}$, $4^{4-6, 30-32}$, 5^{18-20}.

Christian Church. He describes how this has come about; and, in effect, he summarizes what it means to be a Christian: 'Through him [i.e. Christ] we both have access in one Spirit to the Father' (v. 18). This, to the writer and to his correspondents, is the obvious (yet astonishing) description of the Christian life in which they share. The fact that few Christians, and very few non-Christians, would now describe the meaning of 'being a Christian', or of 'belonging to the Church', in this trinitarian manner is both obvious and significant.

A number of theologians have, in recent years, written with commendable clarity and pastoral insight about the doctrine of the Trinity; and their works (if this may be said without presumption) are all-too-rare examples, both in literary style and in content, of the kind of applied theological scholarship which the Churches greatly need. Two of these theologians have described Christian life in terms which aptly paraphrase and illumine the quotation from Ephesians which has just been made.

Leonard Hodgson, after remarking that the Christian follows Christ's example, describes the Christian's life thus:

> He seeks to find and do the will of the Father with the companionship of the Son through the guidance and strength of the Spirit.[4]

Hodgson goes on to remind us that this is not a matter of merely imitating Christ's example; this reproduction of Christ's life in the believer is made possible by God's 'adoption' of him to share in the sonship of Christ; 'thus he shares His Lord's relationship to the Father and the Spirit'. D. M. Baillie expressed the same truth in one luminous sentence: 'The God who was incarnate in Christ dwells in us through the Holy Spirit; and that is the secret of Christian life.'[5]

'That is the secret of Christian life.' The doctrine of the Trinity is an attempt to express the supreme truth about God, and therefore is about matters of which our understanding must necessarily be incomplete; but the most immature Christian is a Christian because God is Father, Son and Spirit, and because of what God does as Father, Son, and Spirit. How far, then, is it necessary for every would-be Christian to learn about the doctrine of the Trinity?

---

[4] L. Hodgson, *The Doctrine of the Trinity*, p. 50.
[5] D. M. Baillie, *God was in Christ*, p. 154.

II. THEOLOGICAL INQUIRY AND CHRISTIAN LIVING

It is tempting to make a clear-cut distinction between thought about the nature of the triune God and faith in Him; but, as has been previously suggested, this kind of distinction is perilous. We are compelled to ask (to express it crudely) to what extent does the ordinary believer need lessons in trinitarian theology? The answer to that question falls into two parts.

1. The need of the believer partly depends upon his individual characteristics: the 'ordinary' believer is a fictional character. Our need for intellectual clarity and the significance of rational thought in our lives greatly vary. It is (I suggest) a safe rule that every Christian should think about the Christian faith at least as strenuously as he thinks about any other subject, not excluding his professional or recreational interests. This need not mean that he should spend as much time on the study of theology as on some other duties; it does mean that he should bring all his powers of thought to bear upon doctrinal study. I do not expect universal agreement with this suggestion, but many years of work among somewhat varied types of people has led me to believe that this is so. Nor should it be imagined that any Christian (save the mentally defective) is too 'simple' to be able to think about the teaching of the Church. If needless obscurity in our teaching is to be condemned, no less blameworthy is our tendency, as preachers and pastors, to despise the intellectual capabilities of most of our flock.

2. The degree of teaching that is needed must be determined with reference to individual and group requirements, but the type of teaching required depends upon the character of the doctrine itself. In academic theology, preaching, and pastoral usage, we are often prone to give priority to the less important and least answerable question. That is especially true about the doctrine of the Trinity.

What it means to God Himself to be triune is a matter which must ever be beyond our comprehension; yet it is upon this question that most discussion of the Trinity (unlike the theology of the New Testament itself) is centred. I do not mean that nothing is to be thought and said concerning this question, but it must be clearly understood that any attempted answer is in the realm of speculation. Ever since Augustine offered a choice of analogies to shed light upon the mystery of the triune Being,

Christians have similarly attempted to clarify their own thought and to help others. So far as my experience goes, most of these similitudes help some people and not others. For example, Dorothy Sayers's use of analogies connected with creative art, in *The Mind of the Maker*, has been found extremely helpful by many of my friends; but I find myself almost entirely unable to grasp her meaning. For many people, including some who would not describe themselves as 'intellectuals', C. S. Lewis's description of the Trinity (in *Beyond Personality*) in terms of 'dimensions' has been (as it has for me) a great aid to thought about God, and later I shall mention another, much older analogy. But speculation of this kind, although it has a place in most Christians' thinking, should have a very subordinate one.

The doctrine which all of us require concerns the triune God's activity. I therefore proceed to make a few comments upon the way in which the doctrine of the Trinity may be taught in pastoral work of all kinds, and I do so by using the traditional terminology: 'Three-in-One and One-in-Three'.

III. 'THREE-IN-ONE AND ONE-IN-THREE'

It is not always appreciated that the doctrine of the Trinity is primarily a doctrine about the Unity of God. (One of the best recent commentaries upon trinitarian doctrine was written by Percy Harthill under the title, *The Unity of God*.) Because of the inflexible monotheism of the first Jewish Christians, and because all that was believed, from the very outset, about the deity of Son and Spirit was affirmed of the One God, the theological controversies of the first four centuries wrestled with the relation of the 'Three' to the 'One'.

Tritheism has been a speculative nightmare, rather than a practical possibility, in the main stream of Christian theology. Yet when we turn to the thoughts and attitudes of ordinary Christians, we are reminded of the need to emphasize the unity of the triune God. There is often found to be an incompatability between men's thoughts about God and their thoughts about Christ. This kind of dichotomy between the character of Jesus and that of the Father is, indeed, not unrepresented among theologians. Charles Wesley, in one of his lapses, represents God, petitioned for mercy, as saying 'Let Me alone', and then giving way because

> My Son is in My servant's prayer,
> And Jesus forces Me to spare,

and some presentations of the doctrine of the Atonement have come perilously near to this fatal error.

In my own pastoral work I had frequently suspected that spiritual difficulties, and even psychological disturbances, were bound up with the existence, in the same mind, of a 'Jesus-picture' and a 'God-picture' which were in conflict. It was therefore with great interest that I learnt that one who has competence to speak about psychological conditions shared this opinion. Ernest White, a Christian physician with considerable theological knowledge, writes: 'I have several times come across this dichotomy in the minds of Christian patients. They are unable to reconcile and fuse the ideas of God the Father and Jesus.'[6] I wish it were possible to quote White's examination of the origin and effects of this dichotomy, and especially what he says about the significance of the child's father-relationship. Here is an example of a psychiatrist who prepares the ground for, and indeed does much of the work of, a Christian pastor; here is an example of the way in which ministers may be encouraged to proceed from where the psychiatrist (*qua* psychiatrist) must finish. Would there were many more such examples!

Repeatedly, then, the pastor will need to help people to replace their false image of God with the likeness of the Christ whom they already seek to follow. Still more often, he will need to turn the attention of those who do not yet believe in God, but who are seeking to discover Him in their own thinking, to Him who is the Image of God.

Many other illustrations might be given of ways in which a separation of the Persons of the Godhead, made unwittingly, adversely affects Christian thought and life. There is often an unrecognized conflict between belief in the Redeemer's goodness and an idea of the indifference (or worse) of the Creator. A belief in the full humanity of the Son of God is uneasily associated with the view that, in God's sight, all that is physical is evil. The Holy Spirit is often depersonalized, thought of as 'It' instead of 'Him', so that mechanistic, and even fatalistic ideas about the Spirit's operations are held alongside trust in the fully personal work of

---

[6] E. White, *Christian Life and the Unconscious*, p. 182.

the Father and the Son. The pastor will find need to interpret in other words the doctrine which the ancient theological language called *perichoresis* or *circumincessio*, the mutual indwelling of Father, Son and Spirit.[7]

There is a very old principle in Christian theology which reminds us that we must not attempt to divide Christian experience into clearly-defined compartments which derive from each of the three Persons. The attempt to do this by, for example, treating the work of the Holy Spirit as one which can be recognized as peculiarly His by some process of introspection—whether that work is associated with baptism, conversion, or the so-called 'second-blessing'—always leads to perversion of sound doctrine and to unfortunate spiritual results. Whenever we think about Father, Son or Spirit, our thoughts are directed towards the same God, 'who as the Father hath made me and all the world, who as the Son hath redeemed me and all mankind, and who as the Holy Ghost sanctifieth me and all the people of God'.[8] But there would be no point in the doctrine of the Trinity if the Threeness were not significant; there would have been no such doctrine had it been judged necessary to affirm only the Oneness.

Within the cure of souls it is, therefore, also constantly necessary to be mindful of the whole of the revealed action of the triune God, to recall all that is done by the Father through the Son and the Holy Spirit, or (to express the same truth differently) all that God does as Father, Son and Spirit. In practice, this requires the pastor to be quick to see which aspect of this total work is most needed by those whom he is seeking to help. If it appears presumptuous to hope that a man may thus recognize the need of others, it can only be replied that unless that is possible, pastoral work is wholly impractical. Moreover, it is precisely for this task that the Holy Spirit's power is promised to the Church; it is He who is to take of the things of Christ and declare them to us, and that of Christ's which He declares is the Father's (Jn 16[15]). The pastoral office, it must also be remembered, is the ministry of the whole Church, a representative pastor does not rely upon

---

[7] A very fine example of the way in which difficult doctrine such as this, or the principle to which I refer in the following paragraph (*opera trinitatis an extra sunt indivisa*) can be expounded pastorally to those who are not very advanced in theological study is provided by a posthumously published lecture by D. M. Baillie (see n. 5), p. 56, above).

[8] C. W. Lowry, *The Trinity and Christian Devotion*, p. 77.

his own insight, nor even upon purely individual inspiration.
Therefore it is to be hoped that the fear of encouraging tritheism will not deter us from exploring the manifold riches of the triune God's blessing. I must be content on this point to refer to the many wise comments upon it made by Leonard Hodgson, and I would draw special attention to the passage in which he writes:

> It is one of the conditions of our life here on earth that in our religion God makes Himself known to us not directly in His unity, but in His several Persons. It is better that we should enrich our spiritual life by exploring to the full the possibilities of our threefold relationship to Him than that for fear of tritheism we should impoverish it and never enter fully into the heritage of the Christian revelation. The more progress we make as men who in their earthly thoughts and words and deeds acknowledge the Trinity, the more we shall find ourselves drawn on to worship the Unity.[9]

Hodgson, in other parts of his book, shows clearly that it is not by reflecting merely upon experience, still less by reflecting only upon our own experience, that we can arrive at the doctrine of the Trinity. Even if that doctrine is itself an interpretation of the experience of the whole Church, that experience itself depends upon the teaching of Jesus Himself. We need, rather, to be *taught* about what the triune God has done, is doing and promises to do.

What was said previously about the pastoral duty to turn men's attention to Christ was a way of saying that 'preaching Christ' belongs to every aspect of the cure of souls as well as to public proclamation to the unbeliever. For the pastor, as for the preacher 'gospel' and 'Jesus' must be virtual synonyms, as they are in the New Testament. It is, however, particularly about the work of the Holy Spirit that the need 'to explore to the full the possibilities of our threefold relationship to God' requires emphasis today.

If the saying, 'the Holy Spirit is the anonymous Person of the Trinity', may appear to lack reverence, it is, we may dare to believe, the kind of jest which God will not resent from His children. One of the astonishing facts about the Holy Spirit is that the very Person of the Trinity who appears most mysterious is the One of whose work we know most. There is a sense in which the Holy Spirit is best recognized in retrospect. When some unexpected goodness has shown itself in our own or another's life,

---

[9] Op. cit., p. 180.

or when some moral victory has been won, we are already prepared to learn about Him. When, from unbelief, we come, suddenly or slowly, to sure trust and confidence in Christ, we can recognize the truth that is told us: 'No one can say "Jesus is Lord" except by the Holy Spirit' (1 Cor 12³). And when the wonder of true fellowship becomes a vivid reality to a small group or to a great assembly of Christians, or between those of different races, colours, temperaments or (even) denominations who are together in Christ, then we can look back and recognize the *koinonia* of the Holy Spirit. It is noteworthy that in the pages of the New Testament we scarcely ever find a petition that the Holy Spirit may be given; the writers are too busily occupied in recounting what he does.

It is in this respect that the point which I tried to make on p. 16 becomes crystal clear. Pastoral work consists very largely in making plain to men and women what God has already begun to do in their lives; the Church's theological task in the cure of souls is very largely (though not wholly) the task of reporting. We do not tell men that they will be created, but that they have been created; nor do we assert that they may be redeemed, but that they have been redeemed; nor do we announce that the Holy Spirit will be sent, but that He has been sent. Yet those who have been created need to be re-created, those who have been redeemed can neglect so great a salvation, and it is more than easy to grieve the Holy Ghost. Therefore the task which I have described as 'reporting' is the telling of good news, and the good news consists of promises as well as of records. All that God waits to do is based upon what He has done; that is true both for mankind as a whole and for each individual. But He has committed to His people both the retelling of the past and the offering of the promises; He has given to His Church stewardship of the mysteries of God.

If, then, there is special need to emphasize the Person and work of the Holy Spirit, that is not because He is 'more important' than any other Person, but rather because it is His work which is most often ignored by men, whereas the culmination of God's saving deeds was the sending of Him forth. There is, perhaps, no instance of individual pastoral counselling, nor any of group pastoral activity, in which some one or other of the 'blessings of the Holy Spirit' does not call for special mention and explicit acceptance.

As Lesslie Newbigin has persuasively argued, we must not

THE DOCTRINE OF THE TRINITY 63

allow the fact that 'pentecostal' thought has often been concentrated in sectarian and even heretical bodies to deflect us from the elements of essential truth in 'pentecostal' teaching.[10] Ever since Montanism, the main body of the Church has tended, especially in the West, to fight shy of particular emphases upon the Holy Spirit. This is a tendency even in present-day Methodism, which (in theory) professes special concern about this doctrine. It is not for me to speak of other denominations, but I believe that all that is least admirable about our Methodist life today is traceable to faulty appreciation of the Holy Spirit's work. If that is an erroneous judgement, at least no Christian will deny that all that is good in our common Christian life is due to His power. When it is recollected that the pastoral ministry of the Church is not only a ministry to those outside, but also a ministry of the Church to itself (for all are both shepherds and sheep), we see a little of the magnitude of the Holy Spirit's place in any adequate pastoral theology. A book worthy of that theme is urgently needed.

IV. 'MYSTERIOUS GODHEAD, THREE-IN-ONE'

It is because the doctrine of the Trinity can help us towards God Himself that it is of deep concern to pastors; but to be brought to knowledge of God is not to gain complete understanding of Him. If the doctrine of the Trinity did not speak about the '*mysterious* Godhead' it would be false doctrine.

That there is room for agnosticism in all true Christian faith is realized by all thoughtful Christians; unfortunately, preachers and theologians sometimes obscure this fact by their words and writings. In a book, the title of which I have forgotten, I read of a university professor who, after a lecture about the Trinity, was somewhat effusively thanked for having 'made everthing plain'; to which he replied, 'God forbid!' It is, perhaps, supremely in regard to trinitarian doctrine that the rôle of Christian theology as a means by which the *limitations* to human knowledge are drawn becomes apparent. There is, however, all the difference between mystery and mystification.

The New Testament use of the word 'mystery' (*mysterion*) is somewhat puzzling to the novice; it is almost, but not quite, a synonymn for 'revelation'. A mystery, in this biblical sense, is a secret that has been disclosed, but, because that disclosure is both

[10] L. Newbigin, *The Household of God*; see also p. 89, below.

partial and incomplete, it remains mystery—it is a secret, but an open secret. That God is Father, Son, Spirit, One God, the Christian is sure; what that means to God Himself the Christian cannot comprehend and does not (if he is wise) attempt to discover; what this triunity means to us men and women the Church has begun to know, ever seeks to know more fully, and waits to know completely in Heaven.

I do not wish to deny, nor in this place to argue, that within the Church's duty lies the responsibility of some of its members to engage in speculative or philosophical theology. That is not the task of pastoral theology, and those who are called to it, whether or not they also have special concern for pastoral theology, must ever be mindful of the secondary character of their work. To quote D. M. Baillie again, the doctrine of the Trinity 'stands finally for the element of *mystery* in the Godhead'; but, he adds: 'The reason for the gladness we have as Christians is that through Christ and the Holy Spirit we know enough of the nature of God to enable us to trust even the utmost depths of its remaining mystery.'[11] If I may venture so to put it, the mystification about God, which is all that natural man can have, becomes transformed into the mystery of God which His adopted children gladly recognize as they live in their Father's love.

And so the triune God can only be known in love and through prayer. It is the aim of the cure of souls to help men to know God thus. God can only be known in *love*, because He is love, and only those who love know God. This love, without which God is unknowable, is itself the love of God shed abroad in our hearts. If that appears to be a circular statement, the circle is not vicious but life-giving, and it is precisely the doctrine of the Trinity which enables us fully to believe that God *is* love. That fact has often been pointed out by theologians; it is, I think, too rarely recognized by others.

When I wrote earlier about analogies which have been used in reference to the triunity of God, I postponed reference to one of the most familiar—namely, that drawn from human relationships. Students of theology will be familiar with all that has been said for and against both the concept of God as a divine society and the particular description of the Holy Spirit as the bond of union between Father and Son. But suppose we stop short of any

---

[11] *Out of Nazareth*, p. 211.

attempt to explain what is beyond explanation, may we not believe that if God is in any sense personal, this must mean that He is more than a 'solitary-individual'? Many psychologists teach us what the Bible ought already to have taught us, that human beings are only persons in and through relationship with others; 'real life is meeting'. How could God be personal (in any intelligible sense of the word) if there were nothing comparable with human-relationship in Him? How could God be love if He existed in solitary isolation? If we believe that there is analogy between human personality and the divine Being, we should not find it difficult to believe that there is some likeness between the closest of human bonds and the relationship of Father, Son, Spirit. Once we learn that God is love, the doctrine of the Trinity becomes one that we might expect to be true.

In actuality, however, it was only when the fulness of the revelation of Father, Son and Holy Spirit had been received that a man was able to write the words 'God is love'. Nobody could have guessed that God is triune; nobody can believe it who does not, however dimly and faithlessly, know that God loves because He *is* love. The love by which Christians may be united to one another is the fruit of sharing in the love of the triune God (Jn 17^{26}).

It is therefore the pastoral office both to speak about, and to be the means through which is made known the love of the triune God. Trinitarian doctrine is about how men and women can truly live, and therefore it is about how they may truly pray. Creeds ought to be sung; theology should spring from and point to worship. The mystifying trinitarian doctrine ceases to be a mere puzzle when it becomes a plain account of how men pray; the 'mysterious Godhead, three-in-one', proves to be the only God we know at all, because He is the God whom we worship.

No words that I could write on this theme could compare with a memorable paragraph by C. S. Lewis. I give myself the pleasure, and the reader the profit of re-reading some of his words, which seem to me to provide an almost perfect example of pastoral theology, of doctrine in the cure of souls:

An ordinary simple Christian kneels down to say his prayers. He is trying to get into touch with God. But if he is a Christian he knows that what is prompting him to pray is also God: God, so to speak, inside him. But he also knows that all his real knowledge of God comes through Christ, the Man who was God—that Christ is standing beside him, helping him to pray, praying for him. You see what is happening. God is the thing beyond the whole universe *to* which he is praying—the goal he's trying to reach. God is also the thing inside him, which is pushing him on—the motive power. God is also the road or bridge along which he is being pushed to that goal. So that the whole threefold life of the three-personal Being is actually going on in that ordinary little bedroom where an ordinary man is saying his prayers.[12]

Theology which can thus describe prayer is theology which can help us to pray. Men and women are not saved by our theology, but unless we believe that they are saved by the God whom our theology seeks to describe, we should be wise to abandon spiritual direction in favour of psychiatric advice—or silence.

[12] *Beyond Personality*, p. 17.

CHAPTER FIVE

FROM THE DOCTRINE OF FULL SALVATION

THE previous chapter provided illustrations of doctrine which appears to be very far removed from every-day life but is, in reality, intimately related to it. In this chapter, examples will be offered of the effect of diversity of theological belief upon our understanding of Christian life. It may well be that readers will strongly differ from views which I shall briefly advocate; if that is so, even my errors will serve to show the seriousness with which we must treat doctrinal beliefs.

The term 'full salvation' is one of many terms which convey different undertones of meaning to different groups of Christians. For some it is a term hallowed by use, and lifts the mind to gratitude to God; to others it smacks of sectarian prejudice and emotional extravagance; for yet others it has little content. I propose to give to this term a somewhat wider reference than it commonly bears. Under the title of this chapter we shall consider, (1) the divine work of justification and sanctification, (2) the doctrine of Christian perfection, and (3) the doctrine of assurance or (to use an alternative designation) the witness of the Holy Spirit. Thus, in considering the pastoral implications of belief in 'full salvation', we shall be thinking about the wholeness of God's saving work, about the wholeness of truly Christian living, and about the completeness with which we can 'know that we are saved'.

Before we proceed to the first of these themes, a further comment must be made about the term 'full salvation'. It is characteristic of Paul's teaching that salvation should be spoken of as a process that is taking place (e.g. 1 Cor 1[18]; 2 Cor 2[15]), or as a future hope (Rom 5[9], etc.). The only place in which he refers to Christ Himself as 'Saviour' is Philippians 3[20], where he speaks about our waiting for a Saviour from heaven. We are accustomed today to speak about 'having been saved', whereas Paul writes about our 'having been justified', or 'reconciled' (see Rom 5[9-20]).

There is no necessary contradiction here, but there is a possibility of misunderstanding. The 'future hope' is an essential part of the Christian doctrine of salvation. When we think about individual salvation we must never forget what is yet to be done; we wait for resurrection to eternal life. When we contemplate the salvation of the world we must consider, not only what Christ has already wrought, but also the consummation of His Kingdom.

I do not suggest that it is wrong for Christians to speak about 'having been saved', although we should be much nearer to the New Testament if we spoke about 'being saved'. Perhaps the term 'full salvation' may help us to focus attention both on what has been done and on what lies in the future, and this richer meaning of 'full salvation' will occupy our attention in Chapter 9 (pp. 133ff). Meanwhile, the next section may help to show that there are false as well as true ways in which we may speak of salvation as a finished act.

I. JUSTIFICATION AND SANCTIFICATION

When we speak about justification and sanctification we refer to the work of God Himself; when we discuss the theology of justification and sanctification we consider human interpretations of the divine work. Even the New Testament writers do not set before us a complete explanation of God's dealing with human souls; they proclaim what He does, and only partially describe the manner of His action. Those who do not believe in an infallible Church will not expect theological statements to be inerrant, whether they are statements made by the fathers of the Church or ones made by Christians today. It is well to remember this, for if God could not save men in spite of inadequate theology there would be no hope for any of us. Yet misunderstandings about the nature, and even about the method, of His activity can hinder us in our acceptance of and growth in the grace of God. It is about a few such misunderstandings (as I believe them to be) concerning justifying and sanctifying grace that we proceed to think.

(1) If I were asked to name the one matter which, above all others, most frequently requires discussion in spiritual counselling it would be faith. I need not enumerate all the misconceptions that exist, such as the notion that faith is a substitute for reason or an alternative way of 'believing', the idea that to have faith is to believe what you do not think is true, the attempt to discover some peculiar mental faculty by which we may 'have faith'. The preacher-pastor must ever be on guard lest his words be taken to

confirm these erroneous assumptions. But even when it is recognized that faith, in the Christian vocabulary, means sure trust in God through Jesus Christ—a trust which involves the whole man, because it is a total commitment, the truth enshrined in the phrase 'justified by grace through faith' may still be calamitously misconceived.

This happens if faith is thought of as a human achievement by which God's forgiveness and favour are earned. Of all the false ways of trusting to salvation by works, this is perhaps the most dangerous to the individual's personal welfare. The attempt to 'get right with God' by deeds of charity will, at least, deliver a man from entire selfishness; the hope that the practice of religious rites will secure salvation will, at any rate, bring him in touch with the gospel, the sacraments and the fellowship of the Church; but if faith is thought of as 'MY faith', then a self-centred, introspective and proud type of piety becomes inevitable. John Wesley once wrote:

We do assuredly hold . . . that there is no justification . . . either by faith or works or both together—that is, that we are not pardoned and accepted with God for the merit of either or both, but only by the grace or free love of God, for the alone merits of His Son Jesus Christ.[1]

If 'by faith alone' is separated from 'by grace alone', the former 'alone' (held in isolation from the latter) destroys the meaning of both faith and grace. Pastoral counselling is not the art of focusing men's attention upon their own spiritual achievements; it is the work of turning their minds towards God, who alone creates the faith which is the only condition that He requires from those whom He 'justifies'.

(2) Even when this is made clear about faith, the concept of justification is itself liable to distortion, and that in two ways. Firstly, because in the Christian vocabulary it means precisely the opposite from what it means in general use. 'My justification is that I didn't know the rules.' 'Please permit me to try to justify myself.' But in the language of the gospel, it is the Offended who justifies and it is the guilty who is pardoned. This theme of

---

[1] *The Craftsman*, 1745. I owe the quotation to J. M. Todd, *John Wesley and the Catholic Church*. As I read these words, I said to myself, '*That* was what the Reformation was about', and then I read Todd's own comment, that Wesley's words offer 'a succinct definition of the Catholic doctrine of grace'. Can we both be right in our comments? If so, many thoughts arise in the mind.

forgiveness, however, will be raised in a later chapter, and it is the second misuse of the concept of justification which is more relevant to this section.

If the justifying grace of God is interpreted in terms of 'imputation', and if this word is understood to mean that God 'puts us right with Himself' without making any change in us, accepting us as though we were His obedient children, although we do not become such, then the beginning of Christian life is based upon a fiction, even if that fiction is allegedly grounded in the merits of Christ. It is then that antinomianism (in many forms) becomes possible. Salvation easily becomes conceived as having little relation to morals, and reliance upon Christ appears to involve making Christ's obedience a substitute for my obedience to God (which is *not* part of the truth in the 'substitutionary' theory of the Atonement). If, on the contrary, we believe, with John Wesley: 'At the same time that we are justified... in that instant we are born again, born from above, born of the Spirit', we know that in treating us as 'right' with Himself God begins to make us so. We shall then begin to comprehend the Pauline doctrine of adoption, and John's teaching about the new birth.

In the cure of souls we do well to stress the analogy with physical healing whenever we 'apply' the doctrine of justification. Those who are brought to the good Physician are brought to be healed, not to be treated as though they were well and left wholly sick. The miracle of divine grace—which astounds us every time we view it in another's life almost as much as it did when we first met it in our own—is that this work of healing can begin at once. This moment a man may be estranged from God, the next moment right with Him; today a man may be gripped in the power of evil, and before night falls begin to be free. The Church that loses the expectation that these things can happen has wandered far from the gospel. This is part of the story of salvation; but it is not the whole story.

(3) It is, I believe, supremely about the relation between justification and sanctification that pastoral theology must be concerned. I must introduce this subject by mentioning the teaching of John Wesley.

In *The Rediscovery of John Wesley*, one of the very few important theological works about Wesley, G. C. Cell argued (at great length) that Wesley provided a synthesis between the Catholic doctrine of sanctification and the Protestant doctrine of justification. There can be little doubt that Cell overstated his case, and that at points he misrepresented both Reformation and Catholic theology, but there is much truth in his judgement if it is considered with reference to ways of thinking which may be more loosely described as 'catholic' and 'protestant'.[2] The former tends to identify sanctification and justification, the latter is apt to isolate justification from sanctification. It is with 'protestant' thought alone that I am here concerned.

Although it is characteristic of much 'protestant' piety to treat justification and sanctification as wholly separate from each other, Wesley cannot be quoted in support of such a division. However much there is in Karl Barth's teaching which would have brought criticism from Wesley (a very militant theologian), he would have found himself in complete sympathy with Barth's insistence (in IV.2. of the *Dogmatik*) upon the fact that justification and sanctification are two moments in the one action of God, and with Barth's statement that whilst justification is first in order of origin and presupposition, sanctification is first as end or consequence.[3] 'Repentance', said Wesley, 'is the porch of religion, Faith is the door of religion, Holiness is religion itself.'

The tendency in modern Methodism (and not in Methodism alone) has been to treat the initial stage of God's saving work as the all-important stage, and sanctification as an 'extra'. In the sense that holiness is possible only on the basis of that free forgiveness and restoration to which the doctrine of justification testifies, it is true that justification is primary; to use another description of salvation, the sinner must be born again before he can grow up as a child of God. But he is born to grow; he is justified to be sanctified; he is adopted as God's child that he may grow into the full stature of the manhood of Christ. This is what 'full salvation' means.

In Sermon 85, Wesley wrote words which are often quoted, but sometimes with the omission of the most significant last sentence:

By justification we are saved from the guilt of sin and restored to the favour of God; by sanctification we are saved from the power and root

---

[2] I shall write 'catholic' and 'protestant' when using these terms to describe tendencies rather than particular denominations.
[3] See the valuable summary of this aspect of Barth's teaching by G. W. Bromiley, *Scottish Journal of Theology*, Vol. 10, No. 1.

of sin and restored to the image of God. All experience as well as Scripture shows this salvation *to be both instantaneous and gradual*.

H. Lindström, in *Wesley and Sanctification*, has conclusively shown (as I have previously noted) that, however frequently and significantly in his *Journal* Wesley delighted to record instantaneous conversions, in all his major writings he stressed the gradualness of growth in the Christian life. His controversies about this matter, with Zinzendorf and others, belong to history, but the manifold ways in which Wesley sought to shape the Methodist Societies in order that they might provide for this growth in holiness are part of his legacy to us. Can it be denied that we are only partially using this legacy? If ever Church organization was constructed to aid the pastoral ministry of the whole Church, a ministry whereby believers may be 'built up', it is that of the denomination whose structure Wesley largely determined. Whilst it would be unseemly, and indeed impossible, for me to make comparisons with other Christian communions, there are searching questions that Methodists must ask themselves.

Has our zeal for growth in holiness kept pace with our zeal for conversion? Have our Church activities multiplied to the deprivation of the very features which are most able to help spiritual development? Have we talked so much about holiness that we have left little time for its cultivation? If, to any degree, these things have happened, have they not been due, in part, to our forgetfulness of Wesley's insight into the true relationship between sanctification and justification?

There are two ways in which that insight may be lost. On the one hand, sanctification may be thought of as an additional gift which can only be received at some post-conversion date and which may be received in its entirety once and for all. I do not doubt that sentences of Wesley's may be quoted to support this notion of 'a second blessing'; but I do not think that his teaching as a whole supports it, nor do I believe that, if it did, it would have any firm basis in Scripture or experience.[4] A more common reason, however, for abandoning emphasis upon the need for growth in holiness is a fear of salvation by works. As 'catholics' are

---

[4] J. Baines Atkinson (*The Beauty of Holiness*, Chapter 6) attempts to establish the type of doctrine rejected above. Whilst there is much deep Christian insight in this modest volume, I cannot find any convincing argument in that particular chapter. It will, however, be clear that if this is the truth, very many consequences for pastoral work will follow.

apt to fear any approximation to 'protestant' emphasis upon justifying faith, so 'protestants' frequently fear that they stand on the brink of 'catholic' heresies if they stress the necessity of the means of grace, the practice of charity, or any notion of men's working together with God in the pursuit of holiness. It is feared that such ideas will lead us away from 'by faith alone, by grace alone', and that upon a foundation of trust in God there will be built confidence in our own works.

This is a natural and to a degree a proper fear for a Christian to have, provided that he does not yield to it. So great, however, can this fear become, that a writer whose understanding of the nature of holiness far surpasses that of most of us can quote with warm approval the words of Jean Nicholas Grou: 'The first steps of holiness are won by our own effort, stimulated by grace; the final ones are wholly the work of God.'[5] So far from the truth does this appear to me, that I am tempted to reverse the statement, and to say that, although in the miracle of regeneration man is often unconscious of any activity of his own, the higher steps in the Christian pilgrimage call for increasing effort; but that, too, would be misleading. Always, God takes the initiative and man responds; always, man knows that his response could not have been made without the help of God.

From what has been said it follows that the Christian counsellor needs to be constantly mindful of two pairs of distinguishable but inseparable truths. First, the pair of truths summed up by the terms 'justification' and 'sanctification'. We should not allow ourselves to be mentally chained to these particular words. It is good to remember, for example, how much of the meaning of 'justification' was taught by Jesus in His story of the publican and the pharisee (Lk 18[9ff]). I expect that most preachers have shared my experience of discovering the shocked response that this story, translated into contemporary idiom, can produce from people today. If potential Christians are to be helped to read the Bible intelligibly, they must be helped to comprehend the terminology of Paul, but they are often best introduced to his teaching by the teaching of the Lord whom Paul interpreted.

Sometimes it is the fact of justification about which men most need to think: they are striving, in one of several ways, to find peace with God, to earn His favour, and they sorely need the

---

[5] J. B. Atkinson, op. cit., p. 87.

gospel of unmerited pardon; they need to be helped to cast their burden upon the Lord. Sometimes it is sanctification to which their thoughts need to be turned: they are presuming upon God's forgiveness and resting content with the first-fruits of His love; they need to be encouraged to persevere in the school of Christ.

The other pair of truths of which pastors must ever be mindful is perfectly stated by Paul: 'Work out your own salvation with fear and trembling; for God is at work in you, both to will and to work for his good pleasure' (Phil 2^{12f}). W. R. Maltby used to warn us against seeking a way of salvation 'by an escalator'. Men may fall into that danger, either by forgetting the steep ascent to heaven, or by forgetting God's power which is offered to them for every stage of the journey. Christian life is neither a joyless, unaided struggle, nor a passive acceptance of mechanical transport. All men, at different times, fail in one way or the other; the rhythm of dependence upon God and obedience to Him is not easy to find, and it is part of the pastoral office to help men to find it.

There can be no doubt, however, about the primary necessity. Whether we contemplate the beginning or the development of Christian life, it is about God that we must chiefly think. Speaking to those who ask, 'How shall we begin to be godly that God may begin His work in us?' Luther wrote:

Do you not understand, it is not for you to work or to begin to be godly, as little as it is to further and complete it. . . .

There is no other beginning than that your king comes to you and begins to work in you. . . . You do not seek him, but he seeks you. You do not find him, but he finds you. For the preachers come from him, not from you; their sermons come from him, not from you; your faith comes from him, not from you; everything that faith works in you comes from him, not from you; and where he does not come, you remain outside. . . .

Therefore you should not ask where to begin to be godly; there is no beginning, except where the king enters and is proclaimed.[6]

II. PERFECT LOVE

If it is granted that sanctification is the goal of the work of grace which begins with justification, the eye of the pastor, and the eyes of the flock, must be set on this goal. This emphasis upon the goal

---

[6] *Gospel Sermon, First Sunday in Advent* (I quote from *A Compend of Luther's Theology*, ed. H. T. Kerr, p. 105).

will offend alike both those who lay all the stress upon 'conversion' and those who dread all types of 'perfectionism'.

To the former it is the decisive change from unbelief to belief which alone matters; for them, the all-important distinction is between the saved and the unsaved, and the whole mission of the Church must be governed by that concern. I have already suggested that this outlook inevitably tends to sunder evangelism from the care of the flock, and I shall not repeat what has already been said on this matter. If the argument of the previous section is valid, readiness to recognize the need for growth towards sanctification need in no way diminish the significance of the initial experience.

The fear of perfectionist doctrine is another matter. No student of Christian history can fail to find grounds for this fear, and I believe it is only as the fear is overcome by deeper understanding of Christian holiness that the doctrine of sanctification becomes an indispensable element in pastoral theology, and concern about holiness takes a major place in the cure of souls. Three lines of thought must now be indicated which, if followed further, might help to clarify our understanding of this matter; they concern (1) the ideal of sanctification, (2) the nature of sanctification and (3) the necessity to strive towards the ideal.

(1) To have one's eye on a goal is not identical with reaching the goal. This obvious truth which Paul expressed in familiar words in Philippians 3^{12}, has been too often forgotten.

Having expressed my conviction that Wesley's understanding of the relationship between sanctification and justification is of permanent value, I must add that I fail to understand how anyone who has read all Wesley's discussions about perfection can fail to regret the time that has been wasted and the confusion that has been caused by some parts of them. This ground has been sufficiently covered by R. N. Flew in *The Idea of Perfection*. Attempts to distinguish between different kinds of 'perfection', the use of qualifying phrases which often render statements nearly meaningless, vain efforts to discover in others a 'perfection' which Wesley would never claim for himself—these and other misguided steps by a great man have often been copied by those less gifted. The pity of it all is that Wesley's own true insights have often been lost sight of by concentration upon these other aspects of his teaching. His recognition of the root of holiness in God's free, justifying grace, his emphasis upon the need for all the means of grace through which *growth* in holiness takes place, and his interpretation of the nature of perfect holiness as perfect love—these are teachings which are of profound and lasting value.

I suggest that three thoughts should dominate our minds when we think about sanctification as an ideal: (i) The goal is perfect love, (ii) there is no limit to God's power to lead us to that goal, and (iii) we must press on towards the goal precisely because we have already started towards it. This is normal Christian living, not an extraordinary way for self-selected or specially favoured individuals; neither gratitude that we are saved, nor consciousness of our present unworthiness, nor speculation about the stage of the journey that we have reached, nor fear of the remoteness of the goal, should distract our attention from either the goal or the way to it.

(2) It is therefore more important to consider the nature of Christian perfection than to attempt to assess how near we are to it. That assessment is impossible, because only a perfect man could recognize perfection if he saw it. Those who claim their own arrival at the goal are usually so patently un-Christlike that even the sinful observer may be forgiven for rejecting their claim; if there are those whose claim is matched by the purity of their lives, that is a matter between God and themselves, and it is no business of ours to judge. Our minds must be fixed, not upon our own or other people's attainments but upon the purpose of God for us.

We do well to concentrate our attention upon Wesley's positive descriptions, as, for example, in his *Plain Account of Christian Perfection* in which he wrote: 'By perfection, I mean the humble, gentle, patient love of God and our neighbour ruling our tempers, words and actions.'

If only he had always been true to his own insight! Unhappily, the inadequate conception of sin[7] which often dominated his thought led him to teach a doctrine of 'relative perfection'. It is difficult to refrain from describing this doctrine as 'playing with words'; it easily leads us to accept an ideal that is too low. Moreover, because Wesley found it impossible to recognize sin in motivation that is unconscious, he unintentionally started many of his followers upon a superficial idea of goodness. That we should reach a stage in which we are not conscious of deliberately acting contrary to God's will may appear far beyond what is possible for

---

[7] See p. 114, below. I have dealt with this subject in *The Meaning of Sin*.

ourselves, though it is not beyond the stage that seems to have been reached by some. But what of the sins of 'ignorance', and the unintentional, unrecognized evil motives that spring from the depths of our as yet imperfectly sanctified nature? The pathway to hell may be partially paved with good intentions, but it is constructed also of bad motives which are hidden beneath the surface. It is these hidden depths, this inmost part of our being, which God would sanctify wholly.

Our convictions about these matters will profoundly influence our pastoral theology, but even more important is our conception of 'holiness' itself.

It is well to recall that 'holiness' has become a derogatory epithet on some lips. For other people, a word which was once firmly rooted in man's reverence before the holy God has come to have a significance which is almost exclusively ethical, carrying the notion of morality tinged with religion. The morality suggested by 'holy' has itself come to be conceived as narrowly individualistic even self-centred, joyless and unlovely. When great words descend to petty use, it is worth taking stock.

Perhaps the word 'holy' is almost beyond rescue in popular usage; but what it stands for must be recovered. Only as holiness is seen to be the life of love (*agape*), the love which belongs by nature to God, and which can be shared by those who are cleansed and empowered by the Holy Spirit, can we recapture the meaning of entire sanctification. Only as holiness is interpreted in terms of Christ-likeness, and Christ-likeness is understood as the consequence of sharing in Christ's own life, can the thought of perfect love become clear. Thus a large part of the whole body of Christian doctrine is relevant to the understanding of the nature of the sanctified life. All this theology is of prime importance in the cure of souls.

We must note especially, that if entire sanctification is understood as perfect love, any kind of self-centred morality or individualistic pietism is a negation of true holiness. The indifference to social and political responsibility which often characterizes Church members, the common tendency to concentrate exclusive attention upon the virtues and vices which are least closely related to wider human relationships, and the fact that morality itself appears to many to be a purely personal, private matter—these are signs of a lost dimension in the spiritual understanding of many Christians. Repeatedly the pastor will discover that individuals and groups of Christians need to remake their whole idea of holiness. The hardest—because the truest—criticism that I ever heard made of the contemporary Church was spoken by one of its most widely respected members, who said: 'The trouble about the Church today is that it is better known for its faith than for its love'. The way in which men are intended to recognize that we are Christ's disciples is by seeing how we love one another.

(3) The last comment I wish to make about sanctification concerns the duty to strive after it.

The Christian life may be thought of as a school in which we learn to love. It is regrettable if unhappy memories of our schooldays make that notion suggestive of irksome discipline; schools are meant to be, and often are happy places, but they call for work, and they require teachers. Why should we think it a sign of lack of dependence upon God's grace so to conceive Christian living? Nothing that Jesus ever said gives us ground to think that Christian life is easy, or that it requires less toil, discipline and sacrifice than any other schooling. By His own example, and by His commission to His first disciples, He showed that those who wished to follow Him needed to be taught. It is just because we have but one Master, even Christ, that we who belong to Him can teach each other, and we should not be surprised by the discovery that some persons are especially fitted for the pastor-teaching ministry. But every teacher discovers, unless he is a very bad teacher, that he can only teach those who teach themselves. So is it in the school of Christian love.

If I may press this scholastic simile a little further, we all know, even if it is hard to explain why it should be so, that more important than the work of any individual teacher is that strange phenomenon that we call 'the atmosphere of the school', which vitally affects the quality of the work and the attitude in which it is done. Each local part of the Church of Christ is intended by God to be a school where adults and children can learn to love, with *agape* love, and here also 'the atmosphere of the school' matters more than the skill of any individual. Thus we again see that the pastoral office is that of the whole Church. A community worshipping, thinking, working together, bound together by the Fellowship of the Holy Spirit in a common love for God and for His Son, so that the stronger help the weaker and the older aid the younger in the craft of Christian love—that is the true Church; and that (as many of us have reason to thank God) it sometimes begins to be. In such a Church, 'full salvation' is no mere pious phrase, and holiness is no utopian and somewhat frightening ideal. And when Christians learn to love with a love like Christ's, other people more readily want to become Christians.

III. ASSURANCE

There is no aspect of the Christian teaching about personal salvation which more clearly illustrates the way in which theological beliefs operate within the cure of souls than the doctrine of assurance.

Is it possible for us, not only to be saved, but also to know that we are saved? There have been, and probably there still are, Christians who could only answer that question in the affirmative by rephrasing it. They would prefer to ask, 'Can we know that we are Christians?' and to that query they would reply: 'If you have been baptized you know that you are a Christian.' If that is the only ground of assurance which is possible or desirable, the doctrine of assurance through the witness of the Holy Spirit falls into the background or disappears. I do not for one moment suggest that a necessary consequence of this view is a neglect of pastoral responsibility. On the contrary, it is those who minimize the significance of baptism, and in particular of infant baptism, who are most often in danger of neglecting those who are, physically or spiritually, young lambs in the flock of Christ. But a lack of stress upon the need for individual, conscious assurance does, I believe, affect the working out of pastoral care.

I shall find it easier to discuss this matter from the point of view of Christians who stress the doctrine of assurance, rather than from that of those who do not. Probably Methodists have always been more vocal about this doctrine than many of their fellow Christians. What was Wesley's experience at Aldersgate Street, to which we Methodists so often refer, if it did not include an awakening of assurance? John Wesley had never doubted his membership in the Church of Christ, and long before 14th May 1738 he was a convinced Christian, a zealous churchman in whose life the sacraments held a primacy that was very rare in his day. The 'heart-warming' experience was certainly not a 'conversion' in any of the varied senses in which the word 'conversion' is most commonly used. Although the facts are probably familiar to the reader, let us recall them, for they are by no means understood by many today, not even by some within the Methodist Church.

I have previously commented that there are far more people who know that Wesley's heart was 'warmed' than there are those who know why it was warmed; there are also many who misunderstand Wesley's experience, for there are various ways in which the doctrine of assurance can be wrongly conceived. It is sometimes imagined, for example, that from the date of his 'conversion' Wesley enjoyed unmixed emotions of joy and peace, and an unwavering sense of spiritual confidence. That is far from the truth. Two days afterwards, on 16th May, he was 'buffeted with temptations', which, though they 'fled away', returned again and again. On 18th May he was troubled by fear, but found comfort in Paul's words: 'Without were fightings, within were fears.' A week later he sought advice from a Christian counsellor, being 'in heaviness because of manifold temptations'.

It would be rewarding to follow Wesley's *Journal* further, and to see how he practised in his own life what a pastor must ever be ready to help his flock to do. He turned to the Scriptures and to pastoral counsel from others, and he set himself more devotedly to prayer and to church attendance. Assurance, for Wesley, was no substitute for the means of grace; it involved no final release from temptation, nor even from moods of despondency. These are facts about the Christian life which greatly need to be explained to Christian people, and especially to those who seek the 'blessed gift of assurance'.

Because I believe that this gift is a 'blessed' one and that it may be received, I believe that the false expectations aroused by the hope of a different kind of gift are among the chief hindrances to its reception. It is often when the 'heart' is far from warm that true assurance is most real. In those days of May 1738 Wesley began to understand that fact, as, with much pastoral help from others, he learnt not to attach undue importance to the changing moods of his volatile temperament, recognized that his former practice of Christian duties must be continued with added determination, and knew that the great experience of his life had involved a turning from himself—from his own emotions and achievements—to the all sufficient power of Christ Himself.

Of course that was the meaning of his experience! Had he not written on 14th May itself: 'I felt I did trust in Christ, Christ alone for salvation; and an assurance was given me that He had taken away *my* sins, even *mine*, and saved *me* from the law of sin and death'. If he underlined the 'me' and 'mine', it was because he trusted in Christ, rather than in himself. *That* is how the word 'assurance' came into the Methodist vocabulary. Would that on Methodist lips, and in all Christian minds, it always carried that meaning!

We cannot avoid thinking about a more controversial question. Wesley wrote that he 'felt' he did trust. How far, in the cure of souls, must we be concerned about that *feeling*? If 'felt' meant a purely emotional feeling, we should have to reject that kind of insistence upon feeling (see pp. 45f, above), but Wesley's own experience is sufficient reminder that a deeply-felt conviction is also an intellectual conviction. If we believe something very strongly we inevitably 'feel' about it. We do well to covet, for ourselves and for others, an assurance of salvation which is so confident and wonder-creating that thought, feeling and will are fully involved, but we shall hinder ourselves and others from enjoying that assurance unless all thought, feeling and will are centred upon Christ Himself. The implications of this fact in the cure of souls require careful attention by all pastors.

Are we to assume that the beginning of such assurance will always be comparable with Wesley's experience? If we do assume that, many consequences will follow in preaching, worship, and pastoral activity of all kinds. For myself, I do not believe that we should make that assumption. It was no coincidence that assurance came to Wesley whilst somebody was reading a preface by Luther to an Epistle by Paul. These three men—Paul, Luther, Wesley—were men of essentially the same type and experience; all of them had for long been deeply religious, all had passionately sought moral victory, and all were keenly intellectual. It is, I am convinced, a profound mistake to assume that those who are like these men in none (or in but some) of these ways will necessarily pass through a similar type of spiritual experience. If our pastoral work is directed almost exclusively to those who first struggle 'under the law', we may well make it harder for some to live 'under grace'. I do not think that Wesley himself ever quite recognized how different from himself most men and women were.

Thus our approach to pastoral work will be deeply influenced by our concept of the nature of assurance, and by our understanding of the ways in which assurance is given. But these are relatively small matters in comparison with our belief about the grounds for assurance.

The only doctrine of assurance which has any firm basis in the New Testament is one that is rooted in the work of the Holy Spirit. Any teaching about assurance which has more to say about human thoughts, feelings and actions than about the work of the Holy Spirit is dangerous in the extreme. Only a Church which is constantly and profoundly conscious of the Holy Spirit's activity can talk about assurance without encouraging the deadly sins of pride and self-centredness. Indeed, it might almost be asserted that where the Holy Spirit is fully reverenced there is not much occasion to talk about assurance, because He gives it.

It is for this reason that I suggest that we may rightly look for evidence by which we may be 'assured'. I am well aware that it is sometimes said that no evidence should be sought other than the New Testament promises. Some Christians would confine pastoral responsibility to drawing people's attention to scriptural statements, such as those which tell us that Christ died for our sins. But before we rest content with that most important duty, we must recall much else that the New Testament teaches, and especially what it teaches about the Holy Spirit.

A better title for 'the doctrine of assurance' is 'the doctrine of the witness of the Holy Spirit'; the key text is Romans 8[15f]: '.... you have received the spirit of sonship. When we cry, "Abba! Father!" it is the Spirit himself bearing witness with our spirit that we are children of God.' If we compare with this all that John has to say (in both Epistle and Gospel) about the work of the Holy Spirit, we learn that is only through Him that we can own the Lordship of Christ, and only through Him that we can know that we are 'of God'. But John also points us to direct evidence of the Spirit's work: 'We know that we abide in him and he in us because he has given us of his own Spirit' (1 John 4[13]), and Paul shows us that we can recognize the gift of the Spirit by the fruits of His work in our lives (Galatians 5[22ff], etc.).

It is therefore by teaching about the work of the Holy Spirit Himself that those who are particularly called to a pastoral ministry may best prepare people to receive the benefits of His work, among which is His witness that we are children of God. This teaching will be given not only in sermon and address, but also in private interview and, less formally, in almost casual conversation; it will be given most effectively by the corporate worship, and by the shared, daily obedience of the Church which is created and sustained by the Spirit. We need to help each other to realize that when we truly call God 'Father', this is a miracle wrought by the Holy Spirit, and that when we—even we—begin to love with Christ-like love, this is because we have received His greatest gift.

Sometimes, to some of His children, God grants moments of overwhelming certainty that they are His, but I do not think that He wants us to crave for such moments, or that He desires us to teach others to do so. However that may be, pastoral care should never be centred upon those experiences. It is by looking, not inwards to our feelings, but upwards to God, that we become increasingly sure of Him. Otherwise we too easily trust to our own confidence.

> Let me no more my comfort draw
> From my frail hold of Thee.
> In this alone rejoice with awe,
> Thy mighty grasp of me.

No human power, least of all that of our own *self*-assurance, can do for us what was done by 'Jesus our Lord, who was put to death for our trespasses and raised for our justification' (Rom 4^{25}). It is through the Holy Spirit that we are sanctified, and through Him alone that we can be sure that we are children of God.

Those who share in the cure of souls will ever seek to turn men's thoughts away from themselves to Him who 'is the source of your life in Christ Jesus, whom God made our wisdom, our righteousness and sanctification and redemption' (1 Cor 1^{30}). This is why it is one of the first duties of Christian pastors to know how to get out of the way.

CHAPTER SIX

FROM BELIEF ABOUT THE NATURE OF THE CHURCH

IN all the major denominations today there is much discussion about the nature of the Church, and it is the doctrine of the Church, with the related theology of ministry and sacraments, which is in the forefront of ecumenical conversation.

One result of this ferment of interest deserves consideration before we pass to the main themes of this chapter. During recent years, each denomination has rediscovered its own traditions and has begun to examine afresh its own concept of the Church. This has directly led to a strengthening of loyalty to particular beliefs, so that it sometimes appears as though the closer the Churches get to each other, the further apart they seem to be. This situation needs to be widely understood if Christians are not to be discouraged. When the nature of the Church (*what* it is) and the existence of the Church (*where* it is) were matters of little moment to many Christians, Christian unity seemed to be comparatively easy. Now that most serious students of Christian theology hold a 'high' doctrine of the Church, differences in belief about the Church become serious obstacles to the furtherance of its unity.

This development should arouse both fear and hope. We must fear lest party loyalty, masquerading as devotion to our heritage, should cause us to confuse prejudice with conviction, to claim exclusive possession of treasures which other Christian communities share with us, and to identify our partial apprehension of the truth with total apprehension. But there is also ground for hope. Two of the causes of the revived and widened concern about the Church are, firstly, zeal for unity, which is, we cannot doubt, the work of the Holy Spirit, and, secondly, fresh study, by Christians in all denominations, of the teaching about the Church in the New Testament itself. The way will not be easy, but there is much to encourage expectations.

There are, however, at least two possible attitudes towards the doctrine of the Church by which Christian unity must inevitably be hindered. They are, on the one hand, neglect or partial neglect of that doctrine, and, on the other hand, exclusive emphasis upon one element in the many-sided truth about the Church. These two false attitudes to the doctrine of the Church (and indeed to any other Christian doctrine)—neglect and narrowness—are especially harmful; it has therefore seemed wise that illustrations of them should be provided in this study of theology in the cure of souls. I have attempted to illustrate the former deficiency in section 1 of this chapter, and the latter in sections 2 and 3.

1. THE CHURCH AND THE GOSPEL

Young students of theology find it almost impossible to believe that there was a time when some Christians paid little attention to the nature of the Church. Yet it was so. At the turn of this century, in what probably still remains the best one-volume work on systematic theology written by a Methodist, W. N. Clarke's *Outline of Christian Theology*, there is only one reference, less than a page in length, to the Church. To go further back, George S. Hendry has reminded us there is no question about the Church in the Shorter Catechism, and that there is no section on the Holy Spirit in the *Westminster Confession* (original form). Today, when books about the Church are pouring into our libraries, and when indifference to the Church by those outside is matched by something approaching an obsession concerning its significance among Christians, it is difficult to realize the change that has taken place.

It is always easy to exaggerate diversities between the thought of one generation and another, and it would be foolish and wrong to think that our Methodist fathers, for example, thought nothing of the Church because many of them said little about it; in cynical moments one is inclined to suppose they thought all the more of the Church because they were not always arguing about what and where it was. Moreover, much that is now seen to belong to the doctrine of the Church was formerly studied in other contexts—for example, in reference to the Kingdom of God. Nor can we accept the frequent accusation that the Protestant Reformation involved a purely individualistic concept of salvation, in contrast to a Catholic doctrine of the Church *The Catholicity of Protestantism* (ed. R. N. Flew and R. E. Davies) had little difficulty in showing that this charge cannot be levelled against Luther and Calvin, but, had that little book found space to consider ways in which some 'protestants' misinterpreted both the Reformers and the Bible itself, a different tale would have been told. Although theological writings by members of all the larger Protestant Churches show that a false kind of individualism is rapidly dying, in the every-day life of the Churches it is as yet by no means dead.

There is probably no other Christian doctrine the neglect of which more drastically affects the cure of souls. If God's purpose for men is thought of exclusively in terms of the salvation of individuals, if the nature of Christian health is conceived as consisting in purely private, individual, spiritual prosperity, and if the concept of togetherness is not at the very centre of the pastoral purpose, far reaching consequences follow for individuals, for the Church and for the world. More profitable, however, than an assessment of such consequences is a consideration of the positive results of a realization of the place of the Church in the purpose of God. Three points call for notice.

(1) *The Church Itself is Part of the Gospel.* Thirty years ago, when the doctrine of the Church was largely in eclipse in many Christian circles, I heard, with astonishment, a lecturer assert that there are only two doctrines in the Bible, that of God and that of the Church. To most of us then, this appeared to be nonsense. Whilst we might still hesitate to speak in just that way, few Bible students would now dispute that the two main facts about which the Old and New Testaments address us are: the fact of God and the fact of the People of God. Now that we clearly see the continuity (as well as the equally significant discontinuity) between the old and the new Israel, the central significance throughout the Bible of God's covenant and electing love, and the great sweep of the record of sacred history that tells what God has done 'to purify for himself a people of his own' (Tit 2^{14}), the Church has come back into its biblical perspective.

From that perspective the pastor sees all men, women and children as potential members of the redeemed family of God. No longer can he apologize for inviting them to church, still less will he seek to conceal his desire that they should become members of the Body of Christ. Only when the Church is conceived as a building, or as a purely human organization, or as a mere aid to individual Christian living, does this apologetic note creep into pastoral conversation; only those who have never learnt what the Church is can treat it as a postscript to evangelism. Men need to be rescued from their terrible isolation from each other (which is most terrible when it is isolation in a crowd) and from their bitter antagonisms towards each other: 'Real life is meeting', and it is only in Christ that we really meet each other.

(2) *The Church and the Means of Grace.* As soon as Christians seriously consider the nature of the Church they are compelled to consider the sacraments and all other means of grace. Those of us who prefer to retain the term 'the sacraments' for Baptism and Holy Communion, do not thereby deny other means of grace which, in a broader sense, we may term 'sacramental'.

An impoverished doctrine of the Church is usually accompanied by a diminished appreciation of the significance of the means of grace. No part of the Church has ever taught that God is bound by His sacraments, or that He is limited to prescribed means by which His gracious favour and His Presence are brought to men, but Christian experience has continuously proved that prayer, the reading and expounding of the scriptures, the fellowship of those who are together in the 'fellowship of the Holy Spirit', Baptism and Holy Communion are the regular and essential means of grace. And so, in the cure of souls, these are the supreme means by which we are cleansed and healed; these are the supreme means by which we may receive heavenly nourishment. The gospel includes good news about these.

All these means of grace are both intensely personal and essentially corporate. Even when a man prays in solitude, he is 'in' the whole company of believers. We need, in many of our Churches, far more simple and definite teaching about the means of grace, such as we saw to be part of the catechetical teaching of the early Church (p. 15). No psychiatric counsel, however valuable, and no other teaching, however necessary, can take the place of that teaching. For want of it many Church members have but little understanding of the function of prayer and worship, of preaching and Sunday school instruction, of sacraments and weekday Church gatherings. They have forgotten, or have never known, that within the visible, organized life of the very frail community of the Church are the God-provided means by which the true life of men can be created and sustained. In this way, too, we have tended to forget what the Church is and what it is for; we should not be surprised if those outside have no inkling of its meaning.

(3) *The Church as Evidence of the Gospel.* The most startling and

yet certain fact is that the Church is intended by God to prove by its own life the truth of the gospel. From the beginning, it was the astounding fact that in Christ there was no Jew nor Greek, no bond nor free, no male nor female, which provided the most compelling evidence for the veracity of the Church's message.

Although we must never minimise the place of individual prophets and evangelists in the progress of the Kingdom, Christian history is full of examples of the evangelistic power of true Christian fellowship; history, both distant and recent, provides similar evidence of the negative influence of Christian disunity, disunity both between the Churches and within individual Churches. So long as we are compelled to take our examples of Christian unity from 'New Testament days', the Franciscans, or the Methodist Societies in the eighteenth century, rather than from our Church down the street and from the Churches of our town, we have no right to expect men and women to find it easy to hope that the gospel may be true. If no other reason prompted in Christian minds a passion for unity at all levels, evangelistic concern and pastoral care ought to do so. As we have noted in a different context, God means men and women to know that He loves them because they can see how Christians love one another.

The doctrine of the Church is, then, part of the good news, for the gospel tells how divided human beings are made at-one; the Church is the sphere, the society, the body, the family within which the reign of God is recognized and obeyed, and within which His Spirit works and His grace is freely received; it is, when it is true to its own nature, the witness, which is seen as well as heard, to the gospel that it proclaims.

Such are a few of the ways in which beliefs about the nature of the Church belong to the cure of souls.

II. MANY TRUTHS ABOUT THE ONE CHURCH

Our thought about the Church must always begin with study of God's purpose for the Church, as that purpose is revealed to us in the New Testament. Throughout Christian history, and (as I have already observed) particularly in recent years, there has been much diversity in interpretation of New Testament teaching. Denominational and other divisions between Christians have resulted in a separation of truths which, in fact, belong to each other; one or other element in the biblical account of the Church has been isolated from the whole picture. This is of special concern to those whose theological interest is primarily pastoral, for a one-sided understanding of the Church is bound to impoverish pastoral care.

F. W. Dillistone, in *The Structure of the Divine Society*, has lucidly summarized two descriptions of the Church which are both found in the New Testament, but which have tended to become isolated from each other in Christian thinking. They are the descriptions of the Church as the Body of Christ and as the People of God. As Dillistone remarks, the former is particularly associated with 'catholic', and the latter with 'protestant' theology and popular belief. In present-day Christian life this contrast has become much less strong, but it still exists, and it is, therefore, important to stress that each side of this controversy can claim scriptural warrant.

Another book, showing no sign of awareness of Dillistone's, has carried the exposition a stage further. Lesslie Newbigin, in *The Household of God*, surveys much of the ground covered by Dillistone. He traces, in the Bible and in Christian history, both the organic concept of the Church (the body of Christ) and the convenant concept (the congregation of the faithful), and his treatment is specially valuable for the exposition of what happens when one or other of these conceptions is stressed exclusively.

Newbigin, however, also pertinently suggests that there is a third description of the Church—namely, the community of the Holy Spirit—and this he describes as the 'pentecostal' point of view, in contrast to the 'catholic' and 'protestant' views. He makes a strong appeal that this third understanding of the Church should gain a greater hearing in ecumenical discussion, for it tends to be the special concern of groups of Christians who are not within the main stream of Christian tradition. This partial exclusion of the 'pentecostal' view is detrimental to both those who hold it and those who neglect it.

Neither of these authors would wish their readers to conclude that there are in the New Testament itself three separable doctrines of the Church, and it is perhaps possible to exaggerate the degree to which the three aspects of the one truth have become separated in the Churches. It is certainly imperative to hold them together, and all who are deeply involved in the Church's life will find reward in a study of these books, and of the scriptural references that they supply. I must limit my comments to a few practical suggestions about the relevance of this kind of study to the cure of souls.

The organic conception emphasizes the wholeness of the Church, which may be described as a body, a temple, a growing building, etc. The covenant idea reminds us that the Church is a people or family, which is called into being by God. The fellowship (or community) of the Holy Spirit is a description of the Church which draws special attention to the relationship between the members, which is through the Holy Spirit. God's people, Christ's body, the Holy Spirit's community—these are descriptions of the one Church, wholly dependent upon the one triune God. Let us imagine a few pastoral situations in which one or other of these aspects of the truth about the Church needs to be recalled.

Here are some Christians functioning as members of a small group within a local Church or of a large, organized denomination; they are very aware of their individual faith, they believe themselves to be called to be the people of God, and they have close fellowship with each other. But their life is impoverished, and their influence is limited, because they have no sense of the Church's wholeness, of the oneness of Christ's body across time and space.

Or let us picture a devout and sincere believer who seeks pastoral counsel; the reality of his own religious experience is not in question, and yet many of the marks of Christian living are lacking. Is this perhaps because he is a solitary-minded Christian, unmindful of the people of God through whom he has received all that he most values, and with whom he may discover much that he still needs to learn and to receive? Yet again, some Christians are zealous in the service of the Church, but sorely need to learn what it means to belong to a 'body' of which Christ is the only Head; and others are depressed and discouraged because they have understood neither the privileges nor the inevitable conflicts that belong to the life of the people of God.

Illustrations need not be multiplied. There is, I believe, no way in which theology is more directly applicable both to individuals and groups. The truth about the Church is too great for any of us to grasp fully, but we all need to explore that truth, to widen our vision of God's purpose for the Church and to learn how the Church may *be* the Church. Moreover, if, guided by the New Testament, we look for the 'real' Church, we shall be surprised how often we find it, and where it is to be found. All too often, when we speak about either the failures or the successes of the Church, we are speaking about what is not the Church; the self-criticism of Christians is often as far from the mark as are the attacks of those outside. Because the pastoral office includes the Church's care of itself, this painstaking effort after genuine self-criticism is part of that office. Diagnosis is a preliminary to the cure of souls, but disease can only be recognized when the nature of health is understood. When professing Christians examine their corporate life, they are apt to call sickness 'health' and to take comfort in falsely supposing that all is well; were this not so, much of our ecclesiastical activity would be modified and much of our corporate self-complacency would be disturbed.

III. THE HOLY AND SINFUL CHURCH

I have spoken of the need for the Church to criticize its own corporate life, and I cannot believe that any Christian would deny that necessity. Yet we all find it very difficult to hold together the two truths that the Church is holy and that the Church is sinful. This difficulty provides a further example of the way in which fulness of doctrine is needful for pastoral insight.

On the one hand are Christians who are very aware of the sinfulness of the Church, but who are unable to believe that it is, in any but a potential sense, holy. On the other hand are those who, whilst believing that any individual Christian (whatever his status) may be guilty of sin, cannot allow that 'the Church' is anything but spotless. Among those who hold the latter view are some who affirm a doctrine of the 'invisible Church', meaning by this that whilst many (perhaps most) people who outwardly belong to the Churches are sinful, the central core, known only to God, is blamelsss. Differences of this kind affect all that is said about 'the Church', and they are bound to influence pastoral work.

The only holiness that the Church possesses is the holiness of God Himself. In that His people belong to Him, they participate in His holiness and are able to be made holy; but the only Church that exists (on earth) is a visible and as yet imperfect community. *Justus et peccator* is true of the Church, not only of individuals within the Church.

The Church proclaims the judgement of God; but she is also under His judgement; those who are in Christ have been made alive by His Spirit, but they continually need renewal by the same Spirit. 'For the Holy Spirit is the creator of the Church, its Lord and Life-giver, its *reformer and tormentor*, and at last its only resource.'[1] 'The Church', as an Anglo-catholic theologian has said, 'is the body, alike of sin and of glory, at once the object and the instrument of the judgement and salvation of God.'[2]

One of the main consequences of this understanding of the Church's nature will be that continual attention will be paid to the Church's need for renewal, and this will affect pastoral activity in countless ways.

It is unfortunate that, when 'revival' is mentioned by Christians today, reference is almost exclusively to the conversion of unbelievers; eagerly as such conversions are to be sought, it would be better not to speak of them as 'revival'. Revival, or renewal, of a Church does not take place because those outside are brought in, although that may well be one of the fruits of revival, and should be the normal purpose of the Church. Renewal of the Church means renewal of those who are 'inside'. I should like to commend a small book by W. A. Visser 't Hooft, *The Renewal of the Church*, which seems in danger of neglect; there are few other books on this theme.

Visser 't Hooft gives a concise summary of scriptural teaching about the need for, and the way of, renewal, and he discusses how far the early Church maintained that tension between confidence in the new thing that Christ had done and a realization of the need for renewal which was characteristic of the Church at the beginning. He also offers a suggestive summary of alternative opinions on this matter, enumerating them under six heads. The first five are: a denial of any renewal other than a return to antiquity, a limitation of the idea of renewal to that of development, a search for renewal by a complete change of the Church into something 'modern' and new, a postponed hope of renewal at the end of history, and an expectation of immediate and enduring perfection. The sixth view is the one which he himself expounds, and I believe it to be the true one. This view is so succinctly stated that a summary, short of lengthy quotation, would be of little value. A few only of Visser 't Hooft's points can be mentioned.

[1] A. Vidler, *Christian Belief*, p. 73. *My italics*.
[2] Gregory Dix, quoted by Visser 't Hooft, *The Renewal of the Church*, p. 95.

FROM BELIEF ABOUT THE NATURE OF THE CHURCH

Renewal is by God alone; but men must seek for that renewal, primarily by searching the scriptures. Renewal is impossible without repentance, and this repentance must be corporate, not exclusively individual, for sin is corporate as well as individual. Renewal always involves the edification (building up) of the Church, fellowship (*koinonia*) and the carrying out of its apostolic mission.

In sharp contrast with those who identify the Church with the Kingdom of God, Visser 't Hooft says (p. 102) that the church—

needs constantly to be renewed by judgement and repentance. But this is not a reason for despair. For the miracle is the miracle of God's grace, of his patience and forgiveness. The miracle is the faithfulness of God who does not leave his people alone, but continues to work at their salvation. The miracle for which we can never be grateful enough, is that the Holy Spirit continues to plead with the Church, 'Be transformed by the renewal of your mind', and that through him the Church is actually renewed.

This is what makes the pastoral office the service of the Church *to* the Church; and this is why the cure of souls is possible; it is God who renews.

One further implication of the type of doctrine about the Church's nature which has been suggested in this chapter requires special notice. From this point of view, the Church will be thought of as a hospital rather than as a museum.

There is much that is attractive in the latter picture; a museum contains rare and beautiful objects, and it is tempting to think of the Church as containing only rare and beautiful human beings, wholly sanctified by grace. But such a picture is unrealistic and false; there never has been a Church of that sort; all the 'high' teaching about the Church in the New Testament is about Churches as far from perfect as the Church at Corinth. It is far nearer the truth to think of the Church as a hospital, the hospital of the good Physician. There is, indeed, all the difference in the world between being in and outside the 'hospital'; but it would not be a hospital if there were not sick people, recovering people, and (alas!) dying people. May I stretch the simile and add that it would be a strange hospital that had no room in it for babies?

Pastoral work, indeed, begins with infants, with the lambs who are to be shepherded in Christ's flock. We should not minimize the doctrinal divergence between those who practise infant baptism and those who believe that baptism can only be administered to believers. A very different doctrine of the Church is involved by these two positions, which Christians hold with equal sincerity. We must respect the convictions, and attend to the arguments of those from whom we differ, but we cannot be excused if we practise infant baptism without a sure belief in its validity and a concentrated effort to make its meaning plain. If a Christian is fully persuaded by the 'Baptist' doctrine, he should, without hesitation, seek admission to that communion. Those of us who, greatly as we admire very much in the corporate life of those who hold exclusively to believers' baptism, think them to be mistaken, have a great responsibility laid upon us. To bring children to Christ in His Church, to pray that He will accept them and bless them, to count them (as, for example, Methodists do) as 'members of Christ's flock', and then to leave them uncared for, unshepherded, unloved by the Church, is a sin for which we can only implore pardon. It is imperative that we give baptised children opportunity to confirm their baptism.

Perhaps there is no single event in the continuing life of the Church which more truly witnesses than does infant baptism to the reality of God's prevenient grace, by which He always takes the initiative, and upon which we all depend for the first, as for the last, steps in salvation. Yet infant baptism testifies also to the necessity for the ministry of the Church; and the Church's attitude towards this sacrament provides clear evidence of its understanding of its own essential character and mission.

Can it be doubted that multitudes of sincere Christians have forgotten, if they ever knew, what God intends the Church to be, and have, therefore, little appreciation of the true weaknesses and failures of the Church? Which of us, indeed, has more than a partial understanding of these matters? Can it be believed that any denomination holds inviolate the fulness of the truth? It is, I believe, partly by the study and exercise of pastoral theology that we may all discover more completely what it means to live in the membership of the one body, as part of the people of God in the fellowship of the Holy Spirit. Without continuous study of the Bible, we shall not see the light which is yet to break forth from God's work; without costly and loving care of the flock, the shepherds cannot comprehend their own sins and responsibilities.

If Christians become wholly immersed in their own and other people's needs, they see the reality of the Church only through the distorting glasses of human sin, and they re-make the Church in their own image; if theological inquiry becomes divorced from the actualities of daily life, the doctrine of the Church becomes unrealistic and therefore false. Thus we have another illustration of the inter-dependence of theology and Christian experience, and we are clearly reminded again that 'experience' is corporate as well as individual. It is only the Church which is attentive to 'what the Spirit says to the Churches' which can truly *be* the Church.

IV. THE CHURCH AND THE WORLD

We have noticed some of the ways in which indifference towards, and limited understanding of the doctrine of the nature of the Church adversely affect the work of theology in the cure of souls. It is also possible for Christians to distort this doctrine by serious misconceptions of the Church's nature. This happens, as was briefly suggested in the last section, when the Church militant is thought to be perfect, 'without spot or wrinkle'; but it can also occur in other ways.

William Temple's words, quoted by his biographer, have often been repeated: 'All the doctrinal errors of Rome come from the direct identification of the Church as an organized institution, taking its part in the process of history, with the Kingdom of God.' Visser 't Hooft, making this quotation, adds reference to the Encyclical, *Quas Primas* (1925): 'The Church is precisely this Kingdom of Christ destined to cover the whole world';[3] and Reinhold Niebuhr, in *The Nature and Destiny of Man* (Vol. 2), has fully discussed this teaching and contrasted it with that of Protestantism.

But Protestants are not free from errors which can have consequences that can be equally far reaching. Although, with few exceptions, Protestants are not tempted to teach a doctrine which makes the Church appear to be a substitute for the living Christ, they may equally distort its meaning by minimizing the distinction between 'the world' and the Church, or by magnifying that distinction until it involves isolation of the Church from the world.

One of the besetting sins of the Church is worldliness. Anxious to acknowledge their sinfulness, and eager to maintain contact with other sinful men, Christians easily become conformed to this world. I do not need to enlarge upon this truth; it is only too familiar. It is the sheer worldliness of much of our worship, of our

[3] Op. cit., p. 95n.

individual and corporate thought and behaviour, and of the conduct of Church affairs, which make the 'Church' the chief stumbling-block to Christian life and witness. The worst enemy of the Church has always been the 'Church'.

But proper fear of these sins can lead to the opposite distortion—to exclusiveness and withdrawal. The ideal for Christians then becomes a community-isolation. Men are to be rescued from their individual life on islands, but they are to be gathered into a corporate life on islands. Ecclesiastical segregation is, ultimately, the most dangerous of all forms of segregation. The Church exists to serve the world; the world is, in New Testament usage, the world that is lost, sinful, doomed; it is also the world that God so loved and that Christ redeemed. The Church has not fully understood its mission to the world when it has recognized its duty to go out to the world; in a more perilous sense it is called to share its Lord's self-identification with the world.

The whole pastoral approach is inevitably influenced by our convictions upon this matter. The pattern of Church-life, the training of young people, the relation between worship and work, and that between the Christian's so-called religious and secular activities—all these and many other issues will be decided, consciously or unconsciously, by our comprehension of the place of the Church in the world. To one or two of these themes we shall return, but I hazard the opinion that we need to be on guard lest concentration of attention upon the Church's own life proves a hindrance to that life.

It is very easy for theologians who study the nature of the Church to become out of touch with the realities of the Church's existence; it is equally possible for those whose principle duty is to work within the Churches to become absorbed in Church problems. When the Church is too greatly concerned about its own business, it is apt to forget the Master's; when the Church is fulfilling its mission, it discovers itself. It was no accident that it was in the persecuted Church in Europe that the slogan arose: 'The first duty of the Church is to *be* the Church'. When that is said by a Church which is under fire there is little peril of disloyalty to Christ in the name of 'the Church'. It is as true of the Church as of individual Christians that the way to discover one's self is to lose one's self, and that from those to whom much has been given, much is required.

PART THREE

FROM PASTORAL EXPERIENCE TO THEOLOGY

CHAPTER SEVEN

FROM LISTENING TO PEOPLE

SO far, we have considered the scope and significance of the cure of souls and the place of theology within that ministry, and have examined a few Christian doctrines from the point of view of pastoral theology, placing emphasis upon the interdependence of Christian experience and Christian doctrine. This interdependence is so complete that it has been impossible in Part 2, wholly to separate the application of theological understanding to pastoral need from the contribution of pastoral experience to the clarification of doctrine; a relationship which is two-way can only be artificially divided for the purposes of discussion.

Now that we turn, in Part Three, to consider ways in which the exercise of the cure of souls influences theological thought, it will be plain that the selection of particular doctrines is purely illustrative. So closely related are all Christian doctrines that we can speak of Christian 'doctrine' (in the singular); so interconnected are all aspects of human existence—in spite of the disintegration which sickness of body, mind and spirit causes—that it would be possible, in each of the following three chapters, to refer to a great variety of human needs. The wholeness of the gospel is addressed to the potential wholeness of the individual and to the whole of the corporate needs of the human family. Some selection of available material is obviously inevitable, and so we shall consider only a few of the many types of pastoral experience, and for purposes of discussion we shall have to treat them as though they could be isolated from each other.

What does pastoral experience involve? At the very least, it involves (1) listening to what people say, (2) being concerned about the moral situation in which they are, and (3) sympathizing with them in all kinds of suffering and in the face of death. From each of these points of view we shall consider varied characteristics of pastoral theology. In this chapter our interest is in (1), the comments and questions that pastors hear.

No pastoral duty is more urgent, none is more difficult, than that of listening. There are obvious reasons for this difficulty:

most of us prefer to talk; important questions are hard to answer; foolish questions are often asked; the most significant questions can hardly be put into words. Moreover, two particular dangers await the pastor who seeks to listen. The first is that of yielding to the temptation to refashion Christian doctrine by attempting to meet the wishes and the assumed needs of our questioners. Thus we may offer them stones for bread, because they sometimes ask for stones imagining them to be food.

In seeking to avoid that danger we may easily fall into its opposite. All men who hold strong religious convictions, and especially those who desire to be theologically orthodox, are liable to hold themselves aloof from others, afraid that they may be contaminated by the theological confusion and the heretical opinions around them. How easily (we may think) we shall be corrupted by false doctrine! If we listen to what men say, shall we not fail to hear what the Lord says? They do not know what they need, how can they ask the right questions? Surely, it is for us to tell them what they need to ask, whether we speak from the unassailable pulpit or in private exhortation!

It would be foolish to minimise the strength of these erroneous suppositions. Many of the questions that are asked about God are of secondary importance, even if they are not so framed as to be unanswerable. The Bible itself disappoints us if we insist on bringing to it our own questions and refuse to attend to the questions which it asks of us. Our Lord's own example is very suggestive. It is true that He rarely gave a direct reply to a question that He was asked; but that is not by any means the whole truth, for He not only listened intently to what people asked, but also elicited from them further questions. 'What do *you* think?' was one of his customary ways of approach to all sorts of people, and when He answered a question, it was most often by asking another.

Like our Lord Himself, therefore, we need to listen, and to provoke question and comment, for the sake of those who are shepherded. In the educative ministry of the Church we must never forget that people need to learn how to think for themselves; instruction is but a means of encouraging them to learn. Viewed as a healing ministry, pastoral work involves unwearying listening, because only thus can the pastor hope to diagnose, and only in this way can he rightly direct others towards the cure which only

God can make possible. Need we doubt that Jesus Himself listened to people with these ends in view?

But our Lord knew what was 'in' men, and although we can be sure that He, too, learnt about them in this way, we cannot compare ourselves with Him. It is only as we listen that we can even begin to understand how to 'communicate' the gospel. In the ceaseless conversation and writing about 'communication' which has occupied so much time and space in recent Christian conferences and literature, all too little attention has been paid to this particular need. This is not the place, nor am I the person, to discuss why the Churches (in England, at least) make such scant use of modern methods of sociological study, why we continue to make generalizations about 'what people think' whilst paying merely haphazard attention to what they say. More relevant to my present purpose is the fact that theology itself must inevitably be made needlessly obscure if we fail to hear what our hearers are saying.

A personal experience may be permitted. It was not until I had to speak (for many months) to a radio audience consisting chiefly of people who did not attend Church services, that I realized the degree of obscurity in my own theological thought. To be compelled to speak briefly about the atonement to those who cannot be presumed to know the meaning of 'sin', 'grace', or (still less) 'atonement', is a salutary experience. I would venture the opinion that whilst, during the last thirty years, the typical preaching of the Churches has become increasingly centred upon the Bible and the gospel, it has also become progressively less intelligible to the average listener. If that is so, it is not inexplicable. So long as preachers were content to speak about 'Christian ethical principles', and to preach sermons on 'Christianity and this or that' (in which more was said about the 'this' and the 'that' than about Christian doctrine), it was comparatively easy to be intelligible; but when we seek to expound the strangeness of the gospel we undertake a much harder task. We make that task impossible if we fail to listen in order to discover what our hearers are thinking and asking, and what they are not thinking and asking.

The teacher-pastor has not fulfilled his duty when he has spoken the words of Hosea as though he were addressing an eighth-century Israelite; Paul wrote to the people of Corinth, but the word which God spoke through Paul to them He seeks to speak through us to the people of London, Melbourne, Calcutta. These are, I fear, somewhat platitudinous remarks, and this particular book makes little, if any, contribution to the solution of the problems to which these platitudes point; but it was impossible to discuss the rôle of theology in the cure of souls without reference to them.

In the remainder of this chapter I shall select, from the innumerable examples that might have been chosen, three closely-related theological doctrines about which we are compelled to think if we listen to what people are saying. I hope that the reader will clearly understand that I am neither attempting a full exposition of these doctrines nor writing about them in the way in which one would wish to speak about them to those who are unfamiliar with Christian teaching. My purpose is to suggest some of the directions in which Christian theological thought needs to move if we are to respond to the stimulus of 'pastoral listening'. The three doctrines to which I shall refer are those of (I) Creation, (II) the Sacred, (III) Man in the image of God.

I. CREATOR OF HEAVEN AND EARTH

I have already hinted that in listening to what people say we must not fail to note what they do not say. One might almost assert that we can learn more from silence than from speech. This is a point that is well illustrated by contemporary attitudes towards the Christian doctrine of Creation.

We are all accustomed to hearing children ask, 'Who made the world?' 'Who made me?' Yet these are questions which many adults do not ask, and about which, so far as we can judge, they rarely think. That men who do not believe in God should reject the notion of divine Creation is to be expected; it is more puzzling that some of them use the word 'Creation'. But what is a disturbing and, I think, a new phenomenon, is that little interest is now shown in the doctrine of Creation by many who are Christians. It is perplexing to meet young, evangelically-minded Christians who are almost scornful in their attitude to hymns that speak of the wonders of Creation, who describe harvest-thanksgiving services as 'nature-worship', and who even object to 'nature lessons' in Sunday school. There are, I am confident, few major Christian doctrines which occupy so small a place in the minds of some Christians today as that of Creation. How has this come about?

Perhaps the fundamental reason for lack of attention to the doctrine of Creation is the belief or suspicion that scientific progress has made this concept unintelligible. When a prominent astronomer can suggest that the proof of 'continuous creation' would shatter Christian belief, it is not surprising if non-believers are strengthened in their position and if believers feel themselves insecure. Because it is painful to face the possibility of error in religious beliefs, many Christians prefer to push the problem into the back of their minds.

Again, many non-believers are now prepared to admit that the 'myth' of Creation is valuable for those who are religiously inclined although that myth has no relation to actuality, and some Christians are content that the physical world, including human bodies, should be dealt with by 'science', leaving the 'spiritual' world to religion. The less religion has to do with 'earthly' things, they believe, the better. More will be said about that matter in the next section.

Points of view such as these can be recognized by the attentive pastor as he listens to other people; and because he is a child of his own generation, he may well discover traces of them in his own mind. All thoughtful Christians, and especially those who have special responsibility for theological study, are challenged, both by the contemporary attitude to the doctrine of Creation and by the development of human knowledge about the universe, to fresh thought about this doctrine. I wish only to draw attention to three particular questions which are raised by an inquiry of this kind; I can do little more than suggest their importance and complexity.

(1) We must make up our minds about the place and value of what has traditionally been termed *natural theology*. Those who are familiar with professional theological work know how fierce and confused are the battles that have been and are being fought over this matter. Speaking very broadly, Protestant thought now finds little room for natural theology, and little use, in particular, for the alleged 'proofs' of the existence of God. Catholic theology, on the other hand, whether Roman or Anglo-, has a great deal to say about natural theology and about the 'proofs'.

This contrast between Protestant and Catholic thought, which is marked although not absolute, helps to explain a fact which often bewilders Protestants, namely, that many converts to Roman Catholicism testify to the attraction of the emphasis which they discovered upon human reason. It is essential that we should understand this. The Roman Church meets the inquirer with the demand that, by the use of his own reason, he should convince himself of the existence of God and of certain other alleged 'facts' (e.g. the alleged existence of an 'infallible' Church and the identification of Rome with that Church). We, on the other hand, appear to him, by our exaltation of faith, to decry reason.

At an earlier stage I have said something about our understanding of faith (pp. 68f), and I cannot here embark upon a criticism of Roman teaching. Keeping to the specific question about natural theology, I must be content to suggest that three alternative positions may be taken, each of which will directly and markedly influence the teaching and pastoral work of those who hold them.

(*a*) We may hold that belief in the existence of God, and belief about certain of His 'attributes', can be established to the satisfaction of any intelligent person without reference to the Bible or to any special revelation. This, as I understand it, is the position taken by most Catholic and by a few Protestant Christians.

(*b*) It may be said that *no* knowledge about God, not even a 'probable' belief in His existence, is possible by any other route than dependence upon the Bible and trust in the revelation contained therein.

(*c*) An opinion which some might describe as being mid-way between (*a*) and (*b*) is also possible; it is the one which I myself hold. It says: Belief in the kind of God in whom Christians believe is reasonable, and can be shown to be reasonable. That is not to say that we expect that anybody will come to belief in the Creator, who is the God and Father of Jesus Christ, in any other way than by learning about Him from the Bible and the Church; nor do we hold that any belief in any other 'God' is a substitute for *that* belief. We reject the distinction between 'natural' and 'revealed' theology as being unhelpful; all theology is the result of both God's self-disclosure and man's thinking. 'Reason' is always necessary if any revelation is to be received.

Each of these views will (as I have said) have its influence upon pastoral work. Those of us who hold the last will want to find a place in the teaching of the Church for two features which are now often conspicuously absent: a preparation for evangelism, by which, at varied levels of intellectual argument, there is shown the reasonableness (as contrasted with the assumed irrationality) of Christian belief in the Creator;[1] secondly, a much greater attention, by believers themselves, to the study of the implications of belief in divine Creation. Everything that we believe about the nature and purpose of human life should be deeply influenced by the concept of Creation, but in many Churches very little teaching about this is now given.

(2) The second task that calls for mention is one which must mainly fall upon those with expert knowledge. The concept of Creation itself needs clarification. It is perfectly clear that in the Bible the emphasis is not upon a temporal beginning. But Genesis starts with 'in the beginning', and to modern men this presents problems which were absent from the minds of ancient Hebrew men. Dietrich Bonhoeffer wrote, in his somewhat paradoxical manner:

That the Bible should speak of the beginning provokes the world and irritates us. For we cannot speak of the beginning; where the beginning begins our thinking stops, it comes to an end. And yet the fact that we ask about the beginning is the innermost impulse of our thinking; for in the last resort it is this that gives validity to every true question we ask. We know that we must not cease to ask about the beginning though we know that we can never ask about it. Why not? Because we can conceive of the beginning only as something finite, therefore precisely as that which has no beginning.[2]

Can such thought be translated into terms which may find a place in pastoral teaching? Can we discover a way by which men of our generation may see that, when all that can be said about how the universe has 'begun' and developed has been said, nothing has been said about Creation? Can they be helped to appreciate that no single object within the universe is fully explained until we ask: 'Why should it exist at all?' Can we regain

[1] I believe that this task involves the formulation of what F. R. Tennant, in *Philosophical Theology*, described as a wider form of the old teleological argument. His positive suggestions about the form of this argument have received far too little attention. Whilst the naïve argument of Paley (on which older people amongst us were brought up) has become obsolete, the broader and stronger arguments for the reasonableness (not for the 'proof') of belief in God's existence have been allowed to go by default.

[2] *Creation and Fall*, p. 9.

in our age, the faith that said, 'In the beginning God created', and the faith that wrote about Jesus Christ, 'Through Him all things were made'? These are questions, among others, about which many Christian minds are now concerned, whether they think in terms of 'demythologizing' or in some other way. Some of us who are not persuaded by much that Rudolf Bultmann writes can also recognize that, with evangelical and pastoral zeal, he is attempting a task which is essential to Christian living, and which is, too often, neglected by his critics. It is not *only* by a 'return to the Bible' that the questionings of modern man about Creation can be answered.

(3) In one respect, however, we do need to return to the biblical outlook, and this point leads us to the third task that I wish to mention. The Hebrew belief in Creation, however much it may have been influenced by speculation outside Israel, was the belief of those who already believed in God as the Saviour of their people. It was this *known* God who 'in the beginning created'. For early Christian faith, although God was still the God of Abraham, Isaac and Jacob, the God of the Exodus and of the prophets, it was the fact that men knew Him in the redeeming work of His Son which gave fresh content to their understanding of Creation.

There is much in these facts which is of importance to us. There is value in the belief that all that is owes its existence and nature to the purpose of 'God', even if 'God' only signifies X—the Unknown; to recognize that nothing is *self*-explanatory is a preparation for Christian faith. But it is only when the word 'God' has a full content that belief in the Creator-God has a Christian meaning. This is the degree of rightness in the position of those who hold that it is *only* God the Saviour who can be the Subject of Christian faith; but they go astray when they fail to emphasize that this Saviour God is the Creator.

That was the truth which John and Paul, for example, proclaimed, when they taught that it was through the Word or Son that the Father had both saved and created. The whole notion of Creation goes astray when this is forgotten, for the doctrine of Creation is not chiefly about how things started to be; it is about why they exist and what they are for. A simple-minded Christian had learnt sound Christian theology when he said that after his conversion 'Everything looked different; the people, the fields, the cattle—all looked different.' Unless we are learning and teaching why everything 'looks different' to a Christian, we are failing to learn and teach the Christian doctrine of Creation.

II. THE SACRED AND THE SECULAR

Whilst there are many questions which may serve to remind the pastor of the doctrine of Creation, it will more often be in indirect ways that his attention will be directed to that teaching, and in particular it will be through observing the attitude of people towards the distinction between the sacred and the secular.

In his book, *The Sacred and the Secular*, E. R. Micklem showed how this distinction has often been falsely drawn, and how attempts to deal with these ideas have often been based upon false premises. Briefly, three points of view can be taken, only the last of which can be said to be fully Christian. (1) Everything may be 'secularized', i.e. God may be left wholly out of account. (2) The secular and the sacred may be wholly separated, so that some objects, people, experiences are the one and some are the other. (3) Everything may be viewed as *potentially* either sacred or secular.

(1) The first of these views calls for no comment; this is what we mean by atheism. (2) The second is an outlook to which religiously-minded people are always prone, and it is one that we have already more than once noted. It is against this idea that we must constantly be on guard in our thinking and in our pastoral work. It results in confining God to selected areas of human experience; religion is departmentalized; much that is in the universe, and many parts of human experience, are treated as though they were matters of indifference to God and to believers, or even as though they were evil. It is in this way that the Church becomes isolated from the world, and it is thus that 'religion' becomes a hindrance to human progress of all kinds. The story is plainly written in history, and it is still being written in professedly religious behaviour.

One of the many disastrous effects of this erroneous distinction between the sacred and the secular is that religion itself tends to be secularized. Apart from the fact that a God who is left in a backwater of human life becomes a God who is unnecessary, with the result that his worshippers pass from belief in this limited God to virtual atheism, 'religious' beliefs and practices tend themselves to become atheistic. This may sometimes be seen in corporate worship. Worshippers who shut the world out of the Church's view, who bring to worship few of the realities of every-day life, end by excluding God Himself; worship becomes man-centred. This may happen in many very different ways, some of which have the outward appearance of religious fervour. Those who are, in this sense, most 'other-worldly' are often furthest from the God who made heaven and earth, and who has redeemed the whole life of mankind.

(3) We need, therefore, to recognize that everything (except evil) is potentially sacred, and it is, I believe, by pastoral care, rather than exclusively by preaching, that we may be helped to learn that 'God has made nothing common or unclean'. The Church's responsibility to teach this calls for much experiment and ingenuity, especially in relation to the corporate activities of Christians. We may be thankful that such experiments are taking place. Groups of Christians are meeting to study, and to pray about, the meaning of their faith for their particular employment or for their social service; Christians who differ in political convictions are finding ways of considering together their supreme loyalty to God; in many school chapels (even if more rarely in our normal Church worship) it is being realized that all that man sees and uses in the world, and all that he does in work and leisure, can either be secularized or sanctified.

Careful attention to daily conversation, to expressions of views in newspaper correspondence columns (not least, the revealing columns of 'religious' papers) and other methods may help us to discover opportunities for learning together the true meaning of 'the sacred'. There is, for example, need for much deeper understanding of the Christian doctrine of vocation. Again, the relationship between Christian faith and the appreciation of beauty, the creative work of artists and craftsmen and the activities of industry and commerce are themes to which little attention is paid, save in a few exceptional quarters. Moreover, it is because of absence of strong belief in the creative activity of God, and because of confused understanding of the sacred that many Christians are comparatively uninterested in social and political affairs. Whilst the leaders of the Churches have probably never been more aware of Christian duty in such matters, nor (it may be added) better informed about them, in many Churches the majority of members lag far behind in interest as well as in knowledge. There are still many Christians whose conception of the gospel leaves little place for social righteousness and political action. When the scientist is discovering the secrets of the universe that God has made and that God sustains, when the man of commerce and the man in industry are working together with God, when the farmer is tilling the earth which is the Lord's and sharing in God's productive creativity, when the housewife is making a home to the glory of God, when in all the common acts of daily life men and women are serving the Lord, then nothing is secular except sin; all things become sacred because all belong to God. From questions which we hear and from the lack of interest which we discover we may learn much about our pastoral responsibility in these matters.

III. MAN IN THE IMAGE OF GOD

The doctrine of Creation is about man himself, because man is part of Creation. Whatever fails to interest us men and women, we rarely fail to be interested in ourselves. Spoken or unexpressed questions about ourselves are never far from our minds: Who am I? Why am I? What may I become? One of the causes of the wide appeal of 'existential' philosophy, especially when it is is presented in drama or literature, is that it raises these questions; sometimes, although less often, it also attempts to answer them.

It is, therefore, in relation to man himself, his nature and his destiny, that pastoral teaching about the doctrine of Creation has much to say. Similarly, the right understanding of 'the sacred and the secular' is especially essential to man's thought about himself. All too easily, 'religion' takes the form of treating the soul as 'sacred' and the body as 'secular'. When this happens, man's oneness with all creation is ignored; he comes to think of himself as a 'spiritual being' whose animal characteristics can be ignored, and as one for whom all natural things exist rather than as one to whom God has given a stewardship over the universe, a stewardship of which he must give account. Even when we learn from the Bible that man has a distinctive and unique place within Creation, this is often taken to mean that he is not a creature, one subject to the law of Creation, but a super-being. At last, man makes himself a 'god'.

Pastoral experience, as well as knowledge of our own temptations to arrogance, compels us to think about the doctrine that man was made 'in the image and likeness of God'.

Although the term 'image of God' is only used three times in the Old Testament (all in Genesis), and less than a dozen times in the New Testament (nearly all by Paul), the influence of this term is much greater, both in scripture and in Christian history, than the few explicit biblical references suggest. Unfortunately this description of human beings has been understood in many conflicting ways.[3] For some, the belief that man is made in the image of God leads to the assumption that man himself, or some part of man, is 'divine'; by others, the image of God is believed to reside in the reason or intelligence of man, which (allegedly) distinguishes him from the rest of creation; by yet others the image of God is thought to be a moral freedom which remains unfettered even in sinful man. I cannot here criticize these different teachings, nor can I stay to suggest the pastoral approaches to which each leads; I must be content to note them, and to urge that we need to make up our minds about them.

There is another way of interpreting the doctrine of man in the image of God which (I believe) is nearer to Christian truth. In this method of interpretation we start, not from Genesis, but from the New Testament, in which (as David Cairns has said) we find three uses of the term 'image of God'. Firstly, it is applied to Christ alone; secondly, to all believers; and thirdly, to all men, even in their sin.[4]

The Son of God is *the* Image of God, and so Jesus is true Man, Proper Man. Behind the word 'image' often lies the simile of a mirror which reflects likeness. The Son is 'just like' the Father. All men were created to mirror the same likeness, but this sinful men, 'fallen' men, fail to do; yet it is still for this that they were created. Those who are renewed through Christ are renewed into that image and likeness, which is their true life. This is the purpose of God: 'And we all, with unveiled face, beholding the glory of the Lord, are being changed into his likeness from one degree of glory to another; for this comes from the Lord who is the Spirit' (2 Cor 3^{18}).

If this be the gospel, all discussion about a 'partial but not

---

[3] A valuable summary of the main theological interpretation has been given by David Cairns in, *The Image of God in Man*, although not all readers will agree with his conclusions.

[4] Op. cit., p. 51.

destroyed' image, and all attempts to discover some aspect of human nature which remains 'divine', become absurd. On the other hand, no human being—not even one's self—can be despised, for all were made to reflect the character of God Himself, and, through Christ by the Holy Spirit, all may become what, by God's intention, they are meant to be. The doctrine of Creation is only intelligible as part of the doctrine of *re*-creation; what man is can only be seen as we recognize what man may be. Whosoever he be to whom the pastoral ministry of the Church is extended, he is one who may reflect the likeness of the God and Father of our Lord Jesus Christ.

The deepest questions of mankind are often too deep for words, but those who have ears to hear will hear them in lesser queries and in the silences of those who dare not speak. They will have no answer unless their own minds are furnished with the fulness of Christian belief, and even with that mental furniture they will know that they only understand in part. Like all true doctrine, the doctrine of Creation points to that which is unknown, as well as to that which has been revealed. But there is all the difference in the world between the worship of an unknown god and the worship of a God whose Name has been made known.

Christian faith is sure that the whole earth is the Lord's and that all human beings are His creatures, but Christian faith also knows, as the ancient doctrine of 'the fall' testifies, that men are strangers, without God and without hope in the world. How can a Christian ever so forget that Man is 'lost' as to think that any man will find it easy to be at home in the world?

Yet another way of thinking about 'the cure of souls' is to think of men's need to be reconciled to earthly life itself. 'Natural' man either seeks to conquer the world, by making it submit wholly to his purposes, or he tries, by one road or another, to escape from it. The Christian religion, as John Oman wrote, is 'distinguished' from all other religions by 'the kind of redemption it offers. In contrast to all ways of renunciation, its way of being redeemed from the world is reconciliation.'[5] When we are enabled to say, 'Abba, Father', we can also say, 'This is our Father's world.'

Now that Oman's words are so rarely recollected, I may close this chapter with further quotation from him:

[5] John Oman, *Grace and Personality* (3rd edition), p. 118.

Graver than lyrical pessimism is the dull rebellion of every day which never hurls impious defiance at heaven and never dreams of offering to curse God and die, which, is indeed, quite piously at enmity with God.[6]

And again,

As enmity against God is primarily enmity against the lives He has appointed for us, because we insist on using them for other ends than His, so reconciliation to God is primarily reconciliation to our lives by seeking in them only His ends. Its immediate significance is *reconciliation to the discipline He appoints and the duty He demands*.[7]

But this reconciliation cannot happen if men refuse to recognize the truth about themselves; for, as Oman also said,

Not till we learn that all things work for evil to those who love themselves and seek their own pleasure and possession in the world, can we discover that all things work for good to those who love God and seek His purpose in the world.[8]

Pastoral care reaches out to men and women who are blinded by sin as well as by ignorance and who are ignorant about their sin, and to that kind of care we now turn our attention.

[6] John Oman, *Grace and Personality* (3rd edition), p. 124.
[7] Ibid., p. 126.   [8] Ibid., p. 117.

CHAPTER EIGHT

FROM CARING FOR SINNERS

IT may appear strange that a particular chapter of a book about pastoral theology should be devoted to the care of sinners. Seeing that all men sin, what other purpose, it may well be asked, has the cure of souls than this? There are, however, several important aspects of the Christian doctrine of sin which have received only fleeting consideration elsewhere in this book. There is also one particular characteristic of human experience which is well illustrated by a study of the care of sinners, namely, the great variety that we encounter as soon as we regard men and women.

'You cannot pack and label men for God, and save them by the barrel-load'; but this is precisely what we are prone to attempt if we look at men in the mass, or approach them with rigid theological presuppositions. When we were thinking about the importance for pastoral care of theology, we repeatedly saw that exclusive, narrow doctrinal beliefs can impoverish that care; now that we are reversing our approach to these two subjects, it must be said that, in a similar way, facile generalizations about human beings can encourage a warped theology, and this may easily injure those whom we seek to help. This will be illustrated in the course of the present chapter, which surveys a somewhat large field.

I. THE SIN-SICK

The term 'cure of souls' focuses our attention upon healing, and the term 'pastoral theology', with its shepherding metaphor, compels us to think of solicitude, of firm but tender care. These terms, therefore, should help to remind us that sin, as the Christian understands it, is a sickness. I believe that we sorely need to maintain this attitude towards sinners, the attitude which was characteristic of Jesus, so that a favourite title for Him has been 'the good Physician'. So essential is it that this care for the sin-sick should dominate evangelistic and pastoral ministry that a little space must be given to underlining its importance. In so doing, controversial statements will be made somewhat dogmatically—a proceeding which, I hope, will be excused because of the fact that I have attempted elsewhere to set forth, with some documentation, the doctrine of sin which is here assumed.[1]

We must note, firstly, that an attitude to sin which is exclusively condemnatory is usually accompanied by the false belief that all that is sinful is a matter of conscious, deliberate wrong-doing. This conception of sin has dominated much of the thought of Christians in recent years, but it is, I am confident, quite incompatible with both the biblical account of sin and the facts of human experience. Pastors who hold to this view may fail to recognize the deepest and gravest needs of their flock, and they may easily be held back from the full offer of forgiveness, for fear that men and women will excuse themselves if they are treated as sick, and (still more) if they are dealt with as victims. This is a needless fear. Who has ever met a man or woman who, having known the 'joy of sins forgiven', has sought to excuse his own most grievous faults? But how many people have never hoped for forgiveness because Christ's servants, in their dealings with them, have never shown Christ's compassion!

Secondly, the realization that sin is a disease, albeit a disease which is always in part self-inflicted, leads to recognition of what is often described as the solidarity of sinners. An individualistic description of sin is as inadequate as the purely individualistic idea of salvation at which we have previously glanced. We sin together, and we are both the causes and the victims of other people's sinful behaviour.

However undesirable it is that we should attempt to popularize the readily misunderstood term 'original sin', the facts which that term summarized must be known and dealt with. They are: firstly, the fact that sin is both deliberate and inevitable; and, secondly, the fact that we belong to a sinful race. Only as we appreciate that the terrible sense of isolation to which sin leads is the imaginary solitude of those who in reality are chained together, can we begin to hear the good news that the chains can be broken and that we can live in the family of God together.

Thirdly, medical metaphors are appropriate when we speak about sin because they remind us that our supreme duty is to offer men pardon and release from sin; it is not our duty to judge

[1] Cp. my Fernley-Hartley Lecture (1956), *The Meaning of Sin*.

them. Metaphors from the law-courts inevitably played a large part in Paul's teaching, and they still have some place in Christian theology, but they need careful handling; they are not very often found in the teaching of Jesus, who usually spoke in terms of personal relationships of many kinds. 'Judge not, that ye be not judged' (Mt 7¹), is one of the most forgotten of His few explicit commandments, and the declaration that He Himself came into the world not to condemn but to save (Jn 3¹⁷) has often been ignored. Too often those who are engaged in the cure of souls vainly seek to assess the respective degrees of guilt of those whom they are called to serve.

This eagerness to apportion blame is so strong that it provides one of the chief hindrances to evangelism and pastoral care. How could we judge one another? By what means of observation, and by what scale, could we measure intentions and actions, opportunities and hindrances, and compare one man's sin with another's? And in what way would it help a sinner to know how 'high' or 'low' his name stood in the list of sinners? It is not by the 'more' or 'less' of legal or ethical judgement that the pastor can distinguish between those to whom he is sent.[2]

There is, however, another way of distinguishing between types of sinners, which the pastor may learn from Jesus Himself. It is clear, in the Gospels, that Jesus treated pharisees and scribes in a quite different manner from other people. Others Jesus treated as sick people who needed healing, and as we watch Him dealing with them it is easy to remember that He was the Good Physician; with the pharisees He was severe, harsh, angry and ironical. We do well to mark this distinction, and we must not attempt to explain it away. 'Those that are well have no need of a physician'; that scathing irony sufficiently explains the whole situation.

It is, therefore, imperative that there should be flexibility in our pastoral attitude to sinners, not because some are more guilty than others, but because what some need first is to be brought to recognition of their need, and what others need first is to be given the assurance that their need can be met.

All those who may be likened to the pharisees fall into the first

---

[2] See the fine discussion of this matter by G. Aulén in *The Faith of the Christian Church*, pp. 284ff, and cp. Sir Walter Moberly's Riddell Memorial Lecture, *Responsibility*.

category. They include those who are very like those contemporaries of our Lord, in that they are moral, religious men who are perfectly confident that their good works guarantee them God's favour; they also include those who are ethically minded but have no belief in God, and those whose hardness of heart is due either to moral obtuseness or to delight in evil. It will be seen that there are strange companions in this company, for men as varied as Saul of Tarsus, a twentieth-century ethical humanist and a hypocritical blackguard alike need to be brought to acknowledgement of their true standing before God. Needless to say, the pastoral approach to individuals in this class will greatly vary, but all of them need to be helped to a recognition of their own unworthiness and of their utter dependence upon the free mercy of God.

All men must, of course, come to that same realization, but there are today, as there were in the days of Jesus, many who in some measure *know* their sickness, both those whose sins are many and weigh upon them, and those who are 'not far from the Kingdom' but need to be brought to a full and grateful assurance of God's forgiving love. Did Christ ever treat such men and women as He treated the pharisees and others whose hearts were hardened? It is true that we must all be brought to repentance and faith; it is not true that we must all travel by the same road. As I have suggested in another context, those who never shared the 'pharasaism' of Saul of Tarsus or Martin Luther or the young John Wesley should not be expected necessarily to pass through all the stages of their experience. Again, those who are reaching a high moral standard but are 'without God', are sinners (in the Christian meaning of the word); but God's way with them will not be identical with His way with the morally corrupt.

I believe that much 'evangelical' Christianity has wrongly sought to fix a pattern, almost a time-table, for the work of divine salvation. I was brought up on that pattern, and early in my ministry I was often puzzled because it did not always fit the need or the actual experience of people whom I met. Not all true Christians have passed through a preliminary stage of remorse and anguish about their sins before they accepted God's forgiveness; for many it is the bitter-sweet experience of pardoning love which first begins to show them how much they needed to be forgiven.

Whether or not the fact is to be regretted, few 'case-books' of pastoral interviews have been published. However, one such record was kept and published by Ichabod S. Spencer, a Presbyterean minister in New York, whose two volumes, *A Pastor's Sketches*, were published in 1851-3. I have been unable to obtain them, but copious quotations are made in Seward Hiltner's, *Preface to Pastoral Theology*, and one example from this record is very germane to the point I am making.

Spencer, as Hiltner demonstrates, showed exemplary devotion and patience in his pastoral work, but he approached all his 'seekers' (as he most often called them) with one aim in view. This aim was (in Hiltner's words) to communicate the gospel 'in such a way that the Holy Spirit will make persons into anxious inquirers, and they will turn to God and Christ and find peace, joy, and solemnity in the faith'. Hiltner quotes at length from Spencer's record of interviews with a Mrs N.; even his summary occupies many pages, and in it we listen to Spencer seeking to help a woman, who has passed through sore trials, to find peace in God. Repeatedly he seeks to unveil some particular sin or other 'hindrance' which will account for her condition. Years passed, and the interviews continued, always dominated by Spencer himself, with the same goal in view. Then, one day, a conversation took place, of which I quote a small part.

SPENCER: Is it not strange that you do not love such a God?
MRS N.: I think I do love God, sir.
SPENCER: How long do you think you have loved Him?
MRS N.: Ever since I was a little child. I cannot remember the time when I did not love Him. It has always seemed to me, as well as I know my own heart, that I did love God.
SPENCER: Why did you never tell me this before?
MRS N.: I was afraid you would think me better than I am.
SPENCER: And do you hate sin?
MRS N.: I have always hated it (if I can judge of my own feeling), ever since I can remember.

Hiltner remarks that this conversation 'hit Spencer like a ton of bricks'. Spencer wrote:

I was utterly amazed! Here I had been for years aiming to make conviction of sin more deep, instead of binding up the broken heart! I had been aiming to lead a sinner to Christ, instead of showing her that she was not a stranger and an outcast! I was ashamed of myself!... I felt as if I had been pouring anguish into the crushed heart of the publican, as he cried, 'God be merciful to me as a sinner!'[3]

It is, perhaps, especially in relation to anxiety and guilt-feelings that we need caution lest a rigidly applied doctrinal-scheme should deepen pathological anxiety and a morbid sense of guilt. Imaginative sympathy is demanded of the pastor, and humble reliance upon the Holy Spirit, if he is not to injure the broken reed and if he is to know when to speak a word that is hard to hear. True doctrines can hurt if they are applied in the wrong way, at the wrong time, to the wrong people. When we deal with sin-sick men and women, orthodoxy is not of itself a guarantee of pastoral wisdom.

II. SIN AGAINST GOD

One of the most puzzling of all Christian beliefs is the belief that a man of high moral attainments can be a sinner. Yet this is the meaning of 'sin', for 'sin' is a religious term and has no clear connotation apart from faith in God. We have not described sin when we have catalogued individual sins, that is, offences and trespasses in thought, word and deed. Sin is self-centred unbelief.[4] Therefore, the primary task of the pastor, as of the evangelist, is to bring men and women to God. If those who are engaged in the cure of souls become more interested in sin than in God, they will surely hinder others from recognizing their own sin. A purely moralistic conception of salvation is a greater hindrance to the divine work of salvation than can be easily measured.

We shall consider, in the next section, the companion-truth that an idea of salvation which is non-moral is no less perilous; but, at this place in our study, it is the former danger which requires emphasis. Repentance is not to be identified with remorse; moral improvement, although it is a fruit of saving grace, is not the whole meaning of 'being saved'. It is only as we truly say, 'Against Thee, against Thee only have I sinned', that we really know what it means to be a sinner, and we know nothing about sin until we know that it is God's forgiveness that we need and may receive.[5]

---

[3] Seward Hiltner, *Preface to Pastoral Theology*, pp. 106f.
[4] I have discussed this definition in, *The Meaning of Sin*; it is based on Aulén's definition of sin as 'egocentric unbelief'. See note 2, page 115 above.
[5] Cp. Karl Barth: 'It is in the light of Jesus Christ that darkness as such is revealed and that consequently it becomes evident that man is a sinner, at the same time as it becomes clear in what his sin consists' (*Church Dogmatics*, IV/1, pp. 123f).

Pastoral experience also confronts us with the fact that men and women stand in need of forgiveness in different ways, and somewhat different theological understanding is requisite for different persons. There are those who see no need for forgiveness by God, either because they do not believe in Him, or because they cannot see that it is against Him that they have sinned; there are those who dare not hope that He will forgive them; there are those who think that they can earn forgiveness. I need not enumerate the particular Christian doctrines which are relevant to each of these instances; rather, I would mention two matters which are of pastoral significance in relation to the whole theme of the forgiveness of sin. The first has to do with God's forgiveness, the second with the place of confession by men.

(1) A great many physicians, whose consulting-rooms are for many people today their only 'confessional', have urged upon us preachers the need to declare more plainly the offer of God's pardon. It may be seriously questioned whether modern preachers do proclaim forgiveness as often as they diagnose evil; but however that may be, it is certain that it is upon the fact of God's forgiving grace that the pastoral ministry of the Church should be centred. Sometimes, it is recognition of the intolerable burden of a sense of guilt that calls us back to our mission; at other times, it is the desperate need of those who do not know that they need pardon that cries out for help. But always, two facts about God's forgiveness must be made clear.

(a) When God pardons He also sets us in a right relationship with Himself, a relationship in which alone the good life is possible; pardon always involves the command and the promise, 'Go, and sin no more.'[6] For some people it is the promise of complete pardon which most needs to be stressed; for others it is the implications of that pardon which must first be made clear.

(b) God's forgiveness is always free. This means that God does not require any payment, not even that of prior virtue; but it also means that there is nothing in God which hinders Him from forgiving. We rightly sing with the children, 'He died that we might be forgiven', but He died, not because God was unwilling to forgive or was impeded by some abstract 'justice', but because

---

[6] Vincent Taylor, in *Forgiveness and Reconciliation*, has shown that in the New Testament the word 'forgiveness' does not carry the wider meaning, mentioned above, which it has in Christian theology. He also shows that Jesus Himself made this wider use of the word inevitable. See also *The Meaning of Sin*, pp. 112ff.

I

only the death of Jesus could remove the hindrances in 'the evil powers' and in man himself. He died because God is a forgiving God, not because God is loathe to forgive.[7]

We thus meet again a pastoral duty which we thought about when considering the doctrine of the Trinity (p. 59, above) We must be watchful to recognize, both in our own presentation of doctrine and in the thoughts and emotional attitudes of those to whom we minister, any trace of the notion that God is coerced into forgiveness; this belief makes any acceptance of His forgiveness impossible.

(2) We come to the second matter to be discussed in this section, the place of confession of sin. God requires such confession to Himself, not as a price to be paid for His forgiveness, but as a part of the act of forgiveness. One person can be 'forgiving', but it takes at least two persons to accomplish 'forgiveness'. That is so even in the unique instance of God's forgiveness; but because in that relationship all the guilt is on one side, all the forgiving is God's, and all the acceptance of forgiveness, which includes confession, is man's.

No Christian doubts that confession must be made to God; there is, however, much difference of conviction about the hearing of confessions by men. This controversial question cannot be avoided by those who share in the care of sinners; unhappily, Catholic-Protestant conflict has made it very hard for us to think clearly about it. The few remarks I shall make upon this subject are an expression of my own opinions; they must not be taken as representing the beliefs of most members of my denomination.

Let us reject any suggestion that confession *must* be made to God in the presence of another person; let us deny that ordination confers an *exclusive* right to hear confessions and to declare, to those who are penitent, the remission of their sins. Let it be further agreed that individual confession in the presence of another involves serious risks: the danger of encouraging 'scrupulosity'; the temptation, to the penitent, to think that he can 'wipe the slate clean' as a prelude to further sinning; even the risk that some may be encouraged to trust in the word of man rather than in the Word of God. Let us be mindful of the abuses of 'the confessional', which Protestants have been quick to see in the

---

[7] A suggestive commentary upon this truth has recently been made by G. S. Hendry in *The Gospel of the Incarnation*.

practices of Catholics; and let us retain (if we so desire) our dislike of anything comparable with a 'confessional box'. Having done all that, is there nothing more positive that we can say?

Every minister who is faithful to his duty does, in fact, hear many confessions, and many a lay man (or woman) in our Churches brings to others the assurance of God's mercy. No preacher hesitates to pronounce assurance of God's forgiveness from the pulpit. Why should it be thought less desirable that the word of release should be spoken in private to an individual? Are we right to leave the desirability of private confession wholly to the unaided decision of our Church members? The exhibitionist, the over-scrupulous and the self-pitying will need little encouragement to talk about their sins, although they may be less eager to learn what God's forgiveness means; but the reserved and the frightened, the very humble and the very proud, and those whose sense of guilt is overwhelming, surely need encouragement?

I should like to commend a beautifully written book about this subject, to the English translation of which I had the honour of writing a preface. Max Thurian, a Protestant pastor of the Taizé community, in his book, *Confession*, founds all that he has to say upon the New Testament. Probably many readers will share my inability to accept the whole of the plea that he makes for a revival of sacramental confession in Protestant Churches, but I do not think that any Christian reader can fail to be moved by much that he writes. I am not suggesting that any dramatic changes should suddenly be made in our practices; I am asking that we should consider whether, by our preaching, by our personal attitude to people, by our accessibility (as ministers) to them, and in other quiet ways, we ought not to make it easier for folk to realize that it is a natural thing (in the family of God) for one man to seek another's help in laying his burden before the Lord and in receiving God's pardon and deliverance. I do not suggest that only ministers can share in this privilege of 'hearing confessions'.

Perhaps many of us would find it easier to think about this matter if we thought less about 'hearing confessions', and more about helping others to recognize their need for and their acceptance of God's forgiveness. We who are His servants are not to stand 'between' men and God; but are we not called to help others to Him? We who have discovered how hard it is to accept the truth about ourselves, and how self-deceitful we can be, who have known moments when we were too afraid and doubtful really to believe that God would forgive us, and who thank God for what one of His children did to help us, cannot but be troubled that many men and women today never dream that such help is available for them.[8]

It may well be that what has been said in the last few paragraphs will win favour only from those who could have said the same things better than I have done, but there are two facts about the truth of which no Christian reader will be in doubt. The first is the fact that it is to Jesus Christ Himself that pastors, as constantly as evangelists, must point. The Church itself must never stand in His way. As G. S. Hendry has said,

> Luther discovered that no ecclesiastically manufactured article can take the place of real forgiveness; for real forgiveness is a miracle and can never be anything other than a miracle; and the word of absolution, *ego te absolvo*, is incredible, unless the *ego* be that of Christ himself.[9]

The other fact is that the most compelling invitation to men to receive the forgiveness of God is our readiness to forgive those who trespass against us. To quote Hendry again: 'The grace to forgive is a witness to the grace by which we are forgiven, because it is the same grace; for there is only one grace, the grace of the Lord Jesus Christ':[10] Perhaps the most worth-while, and the most costly expression of care for sinners is that of those who gladly bear a little share of what sin meant to Christ. We dare not listen to another man's confession unless we are prepared for his sinfulness to hurt us.

III. LAW AND GOSPEL

In the previous section (p. 118) I spoke depreciatingly about 'a purely moralistic conception of salvation'. The phrase is a useful one, but it is not entirely free from ambiguity, for if we must avoid equating Christian life with the meticulous observance of moral rules, we must not fall into the opposite error of emptying

---

[8] Since the above paragraphs were written, W. Telfer, in *The Forgiveness of Sins*, has provided a brief history of doctrine and practice from the New Testament period to Reformation. Read along with Thurian's very different book (referred to above), this survey could well provide a basis for reassessment by the Free Churches, as well as by the Anglican Church to which Telfer specially refers. In a restrained but forceful epilogue he reminds us that 'we do nothing amiss in seeking a doctrine of forgiveness that is at once Catholic and Reformed'.
[9] *The Gospel of the Incarnation* p. 158.   [10] Ibid., p. 170.

the word 'salvation' of all moral content. This, too, is a matter which is of considerable importance in pastoral work.

Even a cursory examination of any Roman Catholic book about moral theology will demonstrate the typical outlook of that type of teaching. Detailed examination of particular moral offences, distinction between 'mortal' and 'venial' sins, analyses of intentions and motives, and discussion of particular virtues—such are some of the features of this type of instruction. In comparison with this, Protestant teaching often appears to be—and not infrequently is—vague and relatively silent about specific moral questions. I wish, not to criticize Roman Catholic teaching, but rather to comment upon the need for increased ethical teaching by those who share the convictions which I have previously expressed.

If we hold firmly to the religious definition of sin as enmity towards God, so that we distinguish between 'sins' and 'sin', the former being the fruit or result of the latter, we may very easily underestimate the moral duties of Christian believers. Even the doctrine of the new birth may be misinterpreted, with the result that the 'saved' are considered to be relieved from responsibility for ethical decision and from strenuous moral endeavour.

Paul's teaching about 'the law' is both extremely difficult for the modern reader to understand and intensely relevant to the point now under discussion; I can think of few doctrines which more greatly need to be interpreted today. The ambivalence, or 'two-sidedness', of Paul's attitude towards 'the law', as being both that from which Christ has set us free and that which the disciples of Jesus must (and can) keep, needs to be recaptured by those who have never, like Paul and his contemporaries, felt themselves 'under the law'.

C. H. Dodd, in *Gospel and Law*, has provided a textbook on this theme which might do for Christian thinking today what his earlier book, *The Apostolic Preaching and Its Development*, did for multitudes of us nearly twenty-five years ago. It is unfortunate that what Dodd and others have taught us about the gospel has been allowed to eclipse what they have written about the teaching (*didache*). If we look yet again at the list of catechetical teaching in the early Church (p. 15), we shall see something of both the true relation between gospel and law and the kind of ethical teaching that is needed.

Amongst the many important points made by Dodd is a valuable summary of the difference between Jewish and Christian understanding of the law of God. For the Christian, the law is embodied in a Person rather than in a code; the goal is approximation towards an ideal rather than conformity to a list of rules; the keeping of the Commandments is by an acceptance of God's grace, not by an effort to deserve His grace; the motive for obedience is a grateful desire to respond to God's love rather than an anxious purpose to acquire merit. Every one of these insights may be directly and valuably applied in pastoral work today.

There is particularly urgent need for clarification of the idea of conscience, and in this connection I must refer to a book of quite unusual importance, which is, so far as I can observe, not receiving the attention that it deserves.[11] C. A. Pierce has shown that the word 'conscience' (suneidēsis) is used by Paul quite differently from the ways in which it was used before his day and has been used since. By Paul, conscience is never conceived as being the principal guide to future action, never thought of as an infallible source of information about moral questions. It is, rather, 'the painful reaction of man's nature, as morally responsible, against infringements of its created limits'; that is to say, for Paul, conscience is that which cries, 'Stop'. And so a man must never act against his conscience, not even if his conscience is mistaken. We can therefore understand how, from Paul's point of view, the ultimate goal of Christian life is to be *free* from conscience, to arrive at the situation in which it is never necessary for conscience to rebuke us.

I have given a very inadequate account of Pierce's thesis. The closing pages of his book provide a fine example of the discussion of the pastoral implications of doctrine. I must, however, add a few comments of my own, even although they involve some repetition. Somebody has said that 'the most neglected of all duties is the duty of finding out what one's duty is'. That duty may be most readily avoided by those who imagine that, having become Christians, they have gained complete moral insight, or who think that merely by looking inward at their own 'conscience' they can be sure of knowing what is right. When 'conscience' is used thus, as a name for ethical ideas and emotional attitudes (as it most

---

[11] C. A. Pierce, *Conscience in the New Testament*. I have also referred to this book in *The Meaning of Sin*, pp. 189f.

commonly is used), we must think carefully. The content of conscience (in that sense) is made up of all kinds of elements: customary moral opinions, childhood experiences, ethical ideas of particular groups and personal prejudices. Of all guides to moral behaviour this is the least reliable.

One of the primary responsibilities of the Church is, therefore, the education of conscience. But the educators are themselves learners. Moral decisions cannnot be rightly taken without detailed study of the facts involved in each situation; it is not simply a matter of applying 'Christian principles' to easily-understood moral problems. Christians must be ready to learn from anybody (whether he is or is not a Christian) about the many varied facts which are relevant to any moral issue.

I take one example of what I have in mind. In the Methodist Church there is a 'Christian Citzenship Department'. A great deal of careful, skilled inquiry is made, by the members of this department, of many types of individual and corporate problems. I do not presume to judge the effectiveness of this work (it seems to me to be of a very high order); I am concerned, rather, about the way in which hosts of sincere Christians think that they can by-pass such activity, and can arrive, whether as individuals or in Church assemblies, at rapid moral judgements upon complex questions. It also seems to me that we need greatly to increase the ethical content of our preaching and the provision of opportunity for people to think together, concretely and factually, about their own moral behaviour.

There has been a violent reaction against 'ethical sermons', although somewhat vague condemnation of a few particular actions—war, drink, gambling—still finds a place in much preaching. We have not fulfilled our moral duty when we have somewhat emotionally made, or responded to, negations of this kind. Pastor-teachers of the flock of Christ are summoned to a continuous exploration of the ethical outworkings of Christian faith. The people whom the Redeemer would 'purify for himself' as 'a people of His own' are to be 'zealous for good deeds' (Tit 2^{14}). The pastoral 'care of sinners' cannot neglect the ethical problems and responsibilities of those who belong to the company 'of pardoned sinners, exulting in their Saviour'.

CHAPTER NINE

IN SICKNESS AND IN HEALTH

'THE saintly "Rabbi" Davidson said that when he looked out on the world the first thing to strike him was not the sin but the suffering.'[1] One of the supreme responsibilities of all who are engaged in the cure of souls is to bring them comfort, in sickness and in health, in trial and in temptation, and in the face of death. 'Blessed be the God and Father of our Lord Jesus Christ, the Father of all mercies and God of all comfort, who comforts us in all our affliction, so that we may be able to comfort those who are in any affliction, with the comfort with which we ourselves are comforted by God' (2 Cor 1³ᶠ).

The devaluation of the word 'comfort' is worthy of consideration. As Ivor Brown has wittily put it, 'our comfort needs comforting in the way of Tudor English'. We have forgotten the association of 'comfort' with 'fortify', and this we must remember every time that we speak of the Holy Spirit as the Comforter. It was *this* comfort that the early Church offered, when it included, among the topics of catechetical instruction, preparation for suffering and persecution (see p. 15, item III, c). For Christians today, as for the first Christians, such instruction must be founded upon the truths of the gospel.

In this chapter no attempt will be made to expound the Christian doctrines to which reference will be made; such a task is far beyond the scope of a chapter. Rather, I shall seek to indicate some of the many theological beliefs about which we are compelled to think as pastors, and about which indeed we all need help if we are to live as Christians. Before we set out on that course a preliminary observation must be made.

A danger implicit in the approach to pastoral care which I am suggesting throughout this book is that it should lead us to imagine that the pastoral office is wholly fulfilled by incessant theological lecturing, in public and in private. There is also risk of our assuming that all the deepest needs of men and women can be expressed in clear questions and answered by precise statements. The things that matter most to us often 'lie too deep for

[1] Quoted by John Baillie, *Invitation to Pilgrimage*.

words'; even the Son of God Himself, who is the Word of God, spoke His most profound words by what He was and by what He did; 'when God wanted to utter the secrets of His heart, He was silent on a Cross'. But Jesus did teach, and so must His disciples. Perhaps it should also be pointed out that not only what we say, but what we are and do, is largely determined by what we believe. It is true that a touch of the hand, a 'look', or an attitude of mind expressed in action or by silence, can sometimes carry more meaning to others than any spoken word, but how we 'look' and how we behave depend upon our own inner thoughts and attitudes. It is what we ourselves believe about suffering and death, and about all the vicissitudes of human life, which most decisively determines our influence upon other people. The preacher who is afraid of death cannot comfort, with Christian comfort, those who must die; the pastor who has not come to terms with 'fate' can only speak hollow words about human destiny.

I. SUFFERING

In the opening paragraphs of a book entitled, *Providence: a Theme with Variations*, Roger Hazelton writes:

Our theme in this book is an august and venerable one—the meaning of God's providence as it is bound up with the tangled, often obscure destinies of men and women living in the world. It is the sort of theme which stretches the mind and probes the heart. It leads us into a realm where even the most venturesome and independent thinkers hesitate to tread. Entering it, we soon abandon the palpable securities of everyday experience in exchange for the more rugged terrain of reality itself. . . .

. . . But this same theme has very much to do with the common scenes of daily life. It is here, if anywhere, that God's voice must be heard, his will declared, his ways revealed. In one sense Providence is the homeliest of all our Christian doctrines. . . .

Yet is not this 'homeliest' of doctrines also, today, the most neglected? In what was said previously about the doctrine of Creation, reference was made to this neglect, for Providence and Creation are inseparable doctrines. In my experience, it is rare to hear sermons about Providence or related topics, yet pastoral contacts provide daily illustrations of confusion of mind, uncomfortable juxtaposition of Christian and non-Christian ideas, half-hidden anxieties and conscious fears. It is distressing to discover Christians of long standing who are trying to reconcile totally un-Christian ideas about Providence with belief in the God and Father of our Lord Jesus Christ.

Yet we may well hesitate to embark upon the troubled sea of questions about God and life which begin with the word, 'Why?' The familiar example of our Lord's attitude to the question about the man born blind (Jn 9[1ff]) serves to remind us that most questions of this kind can only be met by different questions, questions which call for very different answers from those that are sought by the questioners. It is certainly no part of the Christian's duty to claim omniscience; indeed, one of the most truly comforting experiences is the realization that men and women of unshakable faith and courage can only reply to many questions: 'We do not know'. But we need to discover what we can and what we cannot know. Recognition of the hard core of human suffering which cannot be explained is very different from either facile attempts at explanation or sheer bewilderment about suffering of every kind.

I think, therefore, that there is great need for a revival of Christian thinking about the doctrine of Providence. We must be grateful for any book, such as the one from which I have quoted, which offers help of this kind, but I am bound to add that several volumes to which I have recently eagerly turned, because they promised guidance to Christian pastors, seem to me to contain general psychological 'uplift' rather than deeply Christian thought and counsel.

Perhaps the most essential duty of the Church, in relation to teaching about suffering, is one that may best be described, by an analogy with medicine, as preventive work. The hour of great suffering, of any kind, is not the hour for didactic instruction; pain-racked bodies and sorely troubled minds are not comforted by theological argument. The tragedy is that, even within the Christian Church, we are caught unprepared by the ills of life, we are surprised when the protecting walls tumble down.

This preventive work must be partially carried out by preaching. Unfortunately (from this point of view) we cannot select our pulpit audience. On nearly every occasion, some worshippers will be overburdened with suffering, so that our well-intentioned words may only add to their pain; hearers who are battling with specific intellectual difficulties will be sitting beside others who may be injured if those particular problems are suggested to them. The kind of work I now have in mind is better carried out in smaller, more homogeneous groups, but there are some pastoral tasks which can also be attempted from the pulpit. These are both negative and positive.

(1) We must seek to remove the widely held belief that suffering is always proportionate to moral desert. This is the almost instinctive attitude of religiously minded people, as is clearly shown in the Old Testament. W. F. Lofthouse (in a small book now out of print) wrote: 'The traditional and "orthodox" Hebrew view of evil was that all suffering is punishment; that of . . . two kinds of evil . . . physical and moral, the first is the result of the second.' Every pastor meets this view and the utter bewilderment about the facts of experience to which it leads. That God sends His rain on the just and unjust alike is a fact which many non-Christians deem to be a justification for atheism, and which many Christians find inconceivable.

(2) We need to teach people to expect suffering as probable. It is very difficult to do this rightly, without neglecting the equally imperative duty to teach that suffering, wherever it is met, must be fought against. Wonderful medical progress over disease and (especially) pain, the noble ideal of a Welfare State, and other developments, have made men and women (in some areas of the world) both more sensitive to their own physical and mental suffering and less sensitive to the suffering of others. It is not easy to combine tireless opposition to pain and want of all kinds with acceptance of our own burdens; it is not easy to find a way of acceptance which is not that of resignation to 'fate'.

At least two theological questions arise at this point. The first is about what is often spoken of as the 'permissive will' of God, that is, the doctrine that whilst God does not directly will everything that happens, He both permits everything that happens and wills something in it. There are difficulties in this view, as in any alternative view, and I do not propose to argue it here. If however, we reject it, and hold that events happen (whether the 'fall of Adam', or particular human events today, or happenings in nature) which are entirely outside the will of God, we must realize what we are saying. If we save God's moral reputation by invoking some kind of dualism, some belief in an ultimate evil that is over against God, we must (I think) acknowledge that we have abandoned the doctrine of God contained in both Old and New Testaments. If God is, as it were, taken unawares by anything that happens in the universe, if things happen which are not contained in His permissive will, then we must accept all the consequences of belief in that kind of God.

If we take the contrary view, we shall see that the last stand of faith is not the belief that God can remove suffering and evil, but that God permits both because He is love. We may have to say that we do not fully comprehend why He does this; but if, through Jesus Christ, we have a glimmer of understanding of what it means to say, 'God is love', that 'why?' will be hidden in light rather than in darkness.

The second theological question to be mentioned concerns prayer. Should we teach that prayer will always be 'effective' in removing suffering? I know Christians who hold this view, and who believe that if we pray (for ourselves or a fellow-sufferer) with any doubt in our mind about the kind of 'answer' we shall receive, the prayer is less 'availing' than 'believing' prayer. For myself, this opinion is quite untenable, as is the teaching that the number of people praying (or the amount of individual prayer) must have some mathematical relationship with the 'answer' given. I cannot reconcile such views with the teaching and example of Jesus Himself; they seem to me to make nonsense of His own prayer in Gethesemane. All I wish to urge here is that this is the kind of question about which we cannot afford to remain silent.

(3) More important than any of the particular issues so far mentioned, is the total attitude towards life rised by questions about suffering in particular and the ways of Providence in general. This is another reason why the customary separation of Christian belief into individual doctrines is a necessity to be regretted. Every doctrine, from that of the nature of the Godhead to that of the Last Things, has its place within the total Christian view of the significance and purpose of human life. The supplementary title of the American journal, *Theology Today*, 'The life of Man in the Light of God', admirably describes the concern of pastoral theology.

It is in this task of interpreting the whole of life in the light of God that we see particularly clearly why it is that Christian theology can never remain static. However true it is that the fundamental needs of men remain the same, each generation presents fresh situations with which men must deal, offers new opportunities and dangers which they must meet, and provides incentives to a renewed search for the truth which has yet to break forth from God's Word. It is, moreover, in this task that the contribution of laymen, about which more will be said in the next chapter, is most requisite.

Christians must continually seek for both points of contrast and points of contact in the thought, attitudes and behaviour of the contemporary world, and must always recall that they themselves are children of their own generation.

To both hedonistic and utilitarian outlooks, the gospel speaks a word of negation; pleasure, even in its more refined forms, cannot be the ethical standard of those who live within the Kingdom of God; and however productive of human welfare the gospel is, attempts to coerce faith by the promise of benefits to be received must be rejected. As we have previously noted, individualism and collectivism are alike repellent to truly Christian thinking. The desire for 'peace' in the purely negative sense of freedom from trouble, is as contrary to the way of Christ as is war; the Prince of Peace said, 'Do not think that I have come to bring peace on earth; I have not come to bring peace, but a sword'. (Mt 10^{34}). Again, 'this-worldliness' and 'other-worldliness' are terms which describe attitudes to life which are equally contrary to the Christian attitude, and a philosophy of despair is as remote from the outlook of the gospel as is thoughtless optimism.

In the tenth chapter of the Book of the Revelation, a vivid imagery from the prophet Ezekiel is adapted to the Christian message. The scroll of a book which the prophet received, and ate, and found 'as sweet as honey' (Ezek 3^3) becomes a scroll which is taken by the Christian seer, who, likewise, finds it 'sweet as honey'; but (it is added), 'when I had eaten it, my stomach was made bitter' (Rev 10^{10}). The gospel contains good news, but it also contains the 'lamentations, and mourning, and woe' of which Ezekiel wrote. The gospel is always bitter-sweet; those who have never found it hard to 'digest' have not received it. We are in peculiar peril today of concealing the hardness of Christian truth. He who is blind to the wrath of God has never really seen His love; he who fails to understand that we have here no abiding city has not learnt what this world means; he who has never listened to the word about the outer darkness cannot rightly rejoice that the Light has come into the world. Pastors, like preachers, should never be surprised if they and their message are unpopular.

Yet we must also seek for points of contact between the minds of men and the strangeness of the gospel. Where shall we find them better than in the fears and aspirations, the happiness and the pain, of individual and social life? The pastor whose own mind is centred in the Faith will never need to search far to find people who are ready to receive some part of the good news.

Paul Tillich, in all his writings, has urged us to believe that there is today one specially significant point at which the gospel can be communicated. He has expressed this very simply in a paper addressed to Christian ministers and teachers:[2]

Something has happened in our time, which has opened up many people in such a way that we can again speak to them and can participate in their situation. Today there are many people who have become aware of their human existence in such a way that they ask the question to which we can give the answer.

Tillich adds that we shall thus be following the example of Jesus, who, in the Beatitudes, 'points to the situation in which people are and in which they ask for the Kingdom of God.' He reminds us of the anxiety about the meaning of life, fate, guilt and death which is revealed in much of our literature:

Someone has called it 'Wasteland', and others speak of 'No Exit', or 'The Age of Anxiety'. Another speaks of the 'Neurotic Character of Our Times', and another of 'Man Against Himself', and still another about 'Encounter with Nothingness'.

We must not imagine that Tillich conceives that this attitude towards life is universal; rather he suggests that 'we can use these people and their ideas to awaken those among our group who are living in a secure tower'.

Much might be said in criticism of Tillich's argument. Must men always be brought to despair before they can hear the good news? Is it not possible to encourage self-pity and self-absorption in those who are already anxious? Moreover, not all Christians will be able to follow Tillich in his own theological answers to the questions with which he faces us. Yet, I think, we have much to learn from him, especially when he emphasises that we ourselves must neither be identified with the kind of anxiety that we meet in men, nor fail to 'participate in their concern, not by condescension, but by sharing it'.

I should like to make a final quotation from Tillich's book. Having said that there will be as many answers as

[2] Paul Tillich, *Theology of Culture*, pp. 207f.

there are questions and situations, individual and social, he adds:

But there is one thing perhaps which will be common to all our answers if we answer in terms of the Christian message. The Christian message is the message of a new Reality in which we can participate and which gives us the power to take anxiety and despair upon ourselves. And *this we must, and this we can communicate.*[3]

'The message of a new Reality', or (if we prefer to put it so) the message of Reality to all who live in the *unreal*, this is the message which Christian theology seeks to formulate and by which Christians seek to live.

II. HEALTH

A physician is interested in disease because he seeks to restore the patient to health, and health is the primary concern of those who follow in the footsteps of the Good Physician. Christians should have no other interest in sin, whether their own or other people's, than the interest which looks to salvation. 'Love does not rejoice at wrong, but rejoices in the right.' (1 Cor 13⁶). It is, therefore, essential to the cure of souls that there should be understanding of the nature of spiritual health.

It is obvious that physical and mental health are closely associated; it is equally obvious that 'spiritual health' (however that term may be understood) is closely bound up with health of body and mind. As was noted in Chapter 1, the term 'psychosomatic' is as useful to a spiritual director as to a medical practitioner. The precise meaning of the phrase 'physical, mental and spiritual health' is, however, by no means clear. At the present moment, within both the medical profession and the Churches, considerable study is being devoted to this topic, and we eagerly await fuller knowledge. There is widespread and increasing recognition of the fact that the word 'health' is etymologically connected with the word 'whole', and that physical and mental health are interrelated factors in the health of the whole man.[4] There is also a growing, but by no means universal recognition by Christians of the Church's ministry to all kinds of sickness, and of its responsibility for total health.

It is at one limited point that these important matters demand our attention in this chapter. Those who are considering the

[3] Ibid., p. 208.
[4] See *The Church's Ministry of Healing* (Report of the Archbishop's Commission), p. 11.

nature of spiritual health require some standard by which such health may be measured; they need a concept of normality. It is not at all easy to arrive at such a concept. There is, plainly, a close association between this problem and that which faces those whose main interest is in mental (psychological) health.

In his admirable *Pelican* book, *Psychiatry Today*, David Stafford-Clark has reminded us that most people form their conception of what is 'normal' in human experience and behaviour by casual observation. Such observation is usually based upon nothing more than their own limited experience and their own interpretation (or misinterpretation) of that experience. Christians are not excepttional in this respect. We are all prone to judge as spiritually normal the type of piety with which we are most familiar; that is why we find it so difficult to understand other Christian traditions than our own, and that is one of the causes of the extreme conservatism which hinders the enrichment of our worship, our spiritual growth and our comprehension of the things that belong to God. Remedies for this narrow notion of spiritual normality are provided by humble, intimate fellowship with Christians who are very different from ourselves, and by corporate study of the Bible and of a variety of Christian interpretations.

Can we also learn anything from attempts that are being made to give a scientific description of *psychological* normality? Ernest Jones has recently summarized the main contemporary psychological definitions under two heads: (1) those that depend on the criterion of happiness, and (2) those that measure mental health by the individual's adaptation to reality.[5] Each of these tests is applicable by the Christian pastor, although, neither separately nor together, do they provide him with all that he needs.

Happiness is one of the characteristics of Christian life. 'These things I have spoken to you, that my joy may be in you, and that your joy may be full'. (Jn 15[11]). That Jesus came to make us happy is not made plain in every presentation of the gospel. A great many Christian doctrines are relevant to the nature and source of true happiness, but all of them show that happiness is a by-product of a right relationship with God, with other people and with ourselves. Contrasted with happiness is anxiety, which Jones describes as 'the alpha and omega' of psychiatric care. Our

[5] Essay, 'The Concept of a Normal Mind', in *Readings in General Psychology*, ed. P. Halmos and A. Iliffe.

Lord Himself had very much to say about freedom from anxiety, and I have previously cited Tillich's conviction that Christ's remedy for anxiety is for many people their point of contact with the gospel. But this freedom is only the negative feature of mental and spiritual health; one of the many requisites of a sound pastoral theology is a positive account of the meaning of 'blessedness'.

Adaptation to reality, the second test of psychological normality, does not mean (as Ernest Jones comments) that the individual unquestioningly accepts everything in his environment; it means that he is sensitively perceptive of all that is real. Every pastor must learn to recognize the various degrees to which the mentally sick are 'out of touch with reality'; that is, perhaps, the most important part of the psychological training of theological students.

But there is also a much more positive use for this criterion. It has often been remarked that the Bible is a completely 'realistic' book. Unhappily, 'religion' often takes the form of an escape from reality, and that in many different ways. The doctrines of Creation, Incarnation and the Kingdom of God, to cite only a few examples, are beliefs which, rightly understood, compel us to reject many types of facile optimism, 'other worldly' escapism and false ideas about 'spirituality.' Above all, the Christian is confident that to live without God is to live in an unreal world. He can therefore never treat as 'normal' those who are atheists or who worship mental idols. I need not add that to see men as spiritually sick is neither to condemn nor despise them; it should mean that we care for them.

Both happiness and adaptation to reality are useful criteria of normality. Unfortunately some psychiatrists appear to consider it comparatively easy to determine the character of happiness and the nature of reality; some of them interpret these terms in ways that a Christian must reject. (The claim that these issues can be finally decided by the methods of observation which are appropriate to the natural sciences is one which needs to be challenged, although not by me, here.) More valuable, however, than criticism of the opinions of others is recognition of our Christian duty to find out what true happiness is, and to discover what is 'really real'. In that task we must all be engaged, both for our own sake and for that of others. There are ways in which a man may be truly happy although he is far from comfort, ease and ordinary pleasure; he may be psychologically in touch with 'reality' whilst still living in a very 'unreal' world, because he ignores God.

One important point must be added. Christian faith holds that there is a sense in which every human being is abnormal until he accepts the grace of God. It is about this fact that the traditional doctrines of 'the fall' and 'original sin' speak, in words whose meaning it is difficult for us to recapture; it is about this fact that the Christian doctrine of salvation speaks its decisive word. When we think about this, however, we must recollect the variety in Christian spirituality to which I have previously referred. At a superficial glance, sinners are a mixed company and saints a stereotyped class; in actuality, however, it is in Vanity Fair that there is found the dreadful monotony of evil, whilst there is limitless variation among the travellers to the Heavenly City. There can be no mass production of saints; and any attempt at psychological or biological standardization must be resisted by all who care that God's children may be themselves.

Much is rightly said today about the duty of Christian ministers to learn from the physicians, psychiatrists and others who seek to promote health; less is said about the reverse need. Happily there are many instances of co-operation, in study and in practice; but the difficulties are many. In whatever sense theology may be called a 'science', it certainly does not use the methods of the natural sciences; therefore it cannot use the vocabulary which is appropriate to them. Anyone who has taken part in conversation of this kind knows how it tends to proceed on parallel lines which never meet. It is very foolish to suppose that the dispute between science and theology has ceased; all too often it has simply been silenced. Great help by scientists themselves will be needed, if theologians, few of whom have been scientifically trained, are to learn from them. Perhaps our greatest difficulty will be with the growing number of sociologists, psychologists and psychiatrists who, not only (quite properly) pursue studies which are almost entirely physiological in character, but who also assume that theirs is the only way to study man.

Even greater responsibility is laid upon theologians and upon all educated Christians. We have a very great deal to learn from every type of scientist; we have also need to discover for ourselves what it means to think 'theologically' about everything. Very often we assume, for example, that the elements of the Christian doctrine of Man are perfectly familiar to those with whom we converse; sometimes we mistakenly imagine that they are perfectly clear to ourselves.

There is no aspect of human behaviour upon which light is not shed by the gospel. We have failed to say the most important things about Man when we have failed to answer the questions: Who is he, where is he going? No description of either sickness or health can be adequate which does not begin from the wondering enquiry. 'What is man that THOU art mindful of him'? Everything that can be learnt from any source about human nature and human welfare is a matter of concern to Christians, and many individual Christians may share in such discoveries through the social sciences and in other ways. But there are facts about men and women which can only be discovered by attention to the revelation of God in Christ. These are the particular interest of Christian theology. The cure of souls can only be practised by a Church which is continually enlarging its understanding of the truly healthy life of Man. This understanding cannot begin to exist if it is forgotten that men die.

III. DEATH

No better example could be provided of the confusion about Christian doctrine which is common today than that of professedly Christian ideas about death. I think that some ministers of religion would be surprised to discover how many of their Church members hold beliefs in reincarnation, or in the 'immortality of survival in the hearts of our friends'; probably few of us realize how widespread, within our own congregations, is the influence of certain religious sects which have much to say about 'the last things'.

More than a quarter of a century ago, a violent reaction took place in Christian thinking; death ceased to be a matter of primary concern, heaven was pushed into the background, and something approaching a conspiracy of silence about life after death began. No single feature in our worship, preaching and whole attitude to life would more greatly astonish a Christian of any past generation than this. If, to our eyes, some of our Christian fathers seem to have been morbidly interested in dying, we should appear to them to be people who lack that joyful expectation of heaven which dominated their lives. To them, we should seem to be living in an unreal world, a world in which death is not the last enemy, a world in which the last foe has not been vanquished. And they would see us rightly.

I do not need to enlarge upon this subject. The pathetic attempts that are made to cover up the reality of death; the superficial saying: 'It's what happens here, not hereafter, that matters'; the bewildered shock with which Christians, no less than other people, face the imminence of death; the illusory hope that earthly life is bound to continue for ever—these are too familiar to require exposition. Children can grow up, and men and women can become old, within a Church that does not prepare them to die; this is without parallel in Christian history.

It is not easy to rediscover how to preach as 'a dying man to dying men'; it is difficult to interpret the Christian doctrine of resurrection to a generation that no longer shares the thought-forms of the past. The greatest hindrance to the carrying out of this task is the contrast between the Christian doctrine of resurrection (that is, the New Testament doctrine) and the kind of teaching which is popularly desired. In reply to a demand for a scientific proof of survival, the gospel offers a promise of resurrection 'in Christ'; to those who ask for detailed descriptions of life after death, the gospel speaks of a life that is in 'my Father's house'. The entire doctrine of eternal life, as found in the New Testament, is foreign to both contemporary ways of thinking and much professedly Christian belief.

Nor should we minimize the diversity of conviction among serious students of the Bible. This is one of the crucial points at which we must recognize the existence of 'different theologies'. For example, I do not see how the personal convictions and pastoral attitudes of those who hold the doctrine of universalism can fail to differ from those of Christians who reject that doctrine. I am well aware that my own belief that the New Testament provides us with no sure answer to the question, 'Will all eventually enter heaven?' deeply affects my own life and teaching. This situation calls the Church to a more strenuous and devoted attempt to come to a common mind. Again, whilst theological scholars are now busily engaged in studying afresh the eschatalogical teaching of the New Testament, and whilst 'Adventist' and similar groups of Christians are gaining a hearing all over the world, most members of many denominations are left without any teaching whatsoever about the Christian concept of the End of the Age.

I can make only three suggestions about our response to the situation which I have briefly described. (1) Christians who are responsible for teaching of any sort, should never be afraid of acknowledging either their own ignorance or the lack of agreement among Christians. We have, I think, done harm by concealment of this kind; sooner or later, our deception is discovered. (2) We must not, in mistaken kindness, modify what we believe to be Christian truth in order to satisfy the longings of our hearers. (3) We must strive, by preaching, instruction, conversation and the provision of literature, to make known the basic convictions of the Christian Church. I have room only for two examples of the last-mentioned necessity.

Firstly, the doctrine of the resurrection of the body is one which urgently calls for exposition. The fact that, whatever many Christians may have believed, the resurrection of the body does not mean the resuscitation of the earthly body can be clearly demonstrated from the fifteenth chapter of 1 Corinthians. The positive significance of the doctrine can be expounded. The belief that the future life is not a disembodied existence, but one in which there is personal identity and a means of communication with an environment and with other people; and the conviction that it is the total man, not some soul-part of him, which is resurrected—such are some of the meanings of this doctrine. With patience, we ought to be able to speak about these things to the most unlettered.

Secondly (and far more importantly), the truth which is sometimes expressed by the phrase, 'eternal life begins here', must be made known. In this, as in everything that belongs to Christian life, we are brought back again to Jesus Christ and to His Church. The mystifying doctrine of resurrection becomes an open secret to those who have become 'new men in Christ'; the 'company of heaven' has a deep meaning for those who live here in truly Christian fellowship; the Church that truly worships God on earth is conscious of the fact that it is preparing for the worship of heaven, for God has 'raised us up with [Christ], and made us sit with him in the heavenly places in Christ Jesus' (Eph 2⁶).

We who, by grace, have been made members of the Church which is the Bride of Christ are bound to each other and must—

> ... join, with mutual care
> To fight our passage through;

And kindly help each other on,
Till all receive the starry crown.

Learning, teaching and exploring the doctrine of our faith is but one part of that 'mutual care', but if we consider the spiritual weapons with which we are to 'fight our passage through', we shall be in no doubt about its importance. It is with 'truth' that we are to be girded; the sword in our hand is to be the Word of God; and our feet are to be shod 'with the equipment of the gospel of peace'. Our defensive armour—the breastplate of righteousness, the shield of faith and the helmet of salvation—cannot be fabricated by human hands, but if we are to wear this armour we must learn what it is and how we may 'put it on' (Eph 6^{11ff}).

Our main task is now completed. Having made a preliminary survey of the 'cure of souls' and of the place of theology within that 'cure', we examined a few of very many possible examples of the pastoral nature of Christian doctrine. Firstly we considered how theological study can itself direct our minds towards the spiritual needs of ourselves and others. Whilst doing this, we discovered that theological beliefs which at first appear to be far removed from everyday life are, in actuality, concerned with the foundations of Christian living, and we observed ways in which theological misunderstanding injures spiritual progress, and in which diversities of theological insight influence pastoral attitudes. In Part Three, the viewpoint shifted from theology to different kinds of human experience. Attempts were made to illustrate, from some of the needs that all men and women share, the manner in which pastoral care quickens theological concern and may even deepen theological insight.

Much more has been left unsaid than has been expressed. The truth about God is truth about everything; at any moment some fragment of that truth may break into our darkness. The entire Church of Christ, even if it were not marred by division, could not exhaust the truth entrusted to us to be guarded by the Holy Spirit who dwells within us (2 Tim 1^{14}). Although the truth is unchanging, human understanding is always limited and fallible; each generation of Christians is called to explore afresh the truth in which it exists and which it is called to spread. In the closing chapters of this book we shall be thinking about the discharge of theological responsibility within the pastoral ministry of the Church.

PART FOUR

THE PRACTICE OF THE CURE OF SOULS

CHAPTER TEN

THE MINISTRY OF THE WHOLE CHURCH

THE term 'pastoral ministry' has come to signify almost exclusively the work of ordained ministers of religion, carried out in private rather than in public. At various places, in previous chapters, it has been said (usually by way of an aside) that the pastoral ministry is the ministry of the whole Church, and frequent reference has been made to the pastoral aspects of preaching, teaching, etc. I wish now to discuss this wide connotation of the word 'pastoral' more fully.

I. THE WHOLE CHURCH

By the 'wholeness' of the Church' Christians usually mean the organic oneness of all the people of God, that unity or wholeness which is a better definition of the word 'catholic' than is the purely geographical word 'universal'. But part of this essential wholeness of the Church is the oneness of ministers and laity.

There are many indications today of deep concern about this matter. Yves Congar's remarkable volume, *Lay People in the Church*, written by a Roman Catholic, and Hendrik Kraemer's *A Theology of the Laity*, written by a lay theologian from the heart of the ecumenical movement, are just two of many recent contributions to this subject. No less significant is the growth of lay movements within many Churches (to which reference has previously been made), movements which are not anti-clerical, but which seek for closer and fuller co-operation between ministers and laymen. I find it difficult to refrain from too lengthy quotation from writings which describe these movements and discuss the issues involved; I must, however, make some reference to Kraemer's book.

Kraemer reminds us that, in the New Testament, *klèros* (clergy) and *laos* (laity) denote the same people and that these biblical concepts are essentially different from our 'clergy' and 'laity'. All Christians belong to the *laos*, the chosen people of God; all belong to the new community in Christ, 'the body of men and women who share in God's gift of redemption and glory, which is their "inheritance" (*klèros*), because they are incorporated in the

Son'.[1] But 'clergy and laity', as we know these words, have more in common with the 'two sectors of the one body of municipal administration' in the Graeco-Roman city-state: the *klèros* or magistrate, and the *laos* or people.[2]

Kraemer follows the history of this division between clergy and laity until it reaches the full concept of 'two Churches': the hierarchical clergy, who dispense or administer divine grace, and the laity who can only receive what is conveyed to them. Kraemer, however, has not written a polemic against Catholicism; the most valuable feature in his book is the study of the way in which Protestant Churches have also erred in this matter. Luther began by reaffirming the essential oneness of the Church; 'the idea of the clergy as such was rejected.' It is greatly to be hoped that Kraemer's analysis of what has happened in Protestantism since the Reformation will be carefully studied.

Our interest here must be limited to the place of the laity in the cure of souls, and here I quote, once more, John T. McNeill, who reminds us that the cleavage between ministry and laity ought not to have occurred:

What is potentially the most important phase of the Lutheran personal ministry has been the cultivation, as urged by Luther, Bucer and Spener, and widely practised under the influence of Pietism, of the mutual care of souls on the part of laymen. Each man was his brother's keeper in a spiritual fellowship.' '*Seelsorge aller an allen*' (the care of all for the souls of all), aptly expresses this principle.[3]

Methodism is one denomination in which this principle, 'the care of all for the souls of all', was once strongly held and faithfully followed; the Methodist Church would not have survived and grown until now had it been totally abandoned, but all is not well with us.

The ironical fact is that Christians who are most violently opposed to a 'priestly' and hierarchical ministry can make a similar cleavage between ministers and laity. Moreover, to say 'there is no difference between a minister and a layman' is as far from the truth (and the point) as is the kind of division into clergy and laity at which we have just glanced. To make this point clear, something must be said about the doctrine of the priesthood of all believers.

[1] H. Kraemer, *A Theology of the Laity*, p. 52.
[2] Ibid., p. 51.   [3] *A History of the Cure of Souls*, p. 190.

THE MINISTRY OF THE WHOLE CHURCH 145

I have sympathy with Kraemer's plea that, as we seek a truer theology of the laity, we should not make this doctrine our starting point.[4] The phrase itself has come to play a much larger part in Christian thought than it did formerly; it is not found in the New Testament and, although it has an honourable history, it is easily misunderstood. Unfortunately, it has gathered to itself two notions which are quite irrelevant to the truths which it describes. It has come to mean that there is no difference between ministers and laymen, which is obviously untrue; it has also been taken to imply that every individual in his own 'priest', which, if it means anything at all, is also untrue. The former misunderstanding will concern us in the next chapter, but we note the strange way in which the doctrine of the priesthood of *all* believers has come to signify the priesthood of *each* believer.

In the New Testament the word 'priest' is never used about a Christian individual; though it is, of course, used about our Lord Himself. (Similarly, the word 'saints' only appears in the plural.) The whole Church is 'a holy priesthood' (1 Pet 2^5), but even the Church itself is only a priesthood in a derivative sense. There is only one High Priest; there is (to cite T. W. Manson's familiar words) only one *essential* ministry in the Church, the ministry of Christ Himself.

What we have tended to do is to ascribe to every Christian the function of an individual 'priesthood'. This 'priesthood' is then misconceived as being directed to oneself; a man is 'his own priest'. Kraemer remarks that the word *klèros* (clergy) had, in the Church of the second century, 'a point of attachment in the way in which the Old Testament speaks about the Levites or priests, to whom the Lord is "the allotted portion" (*klèros*; Num 18^{20})'. There is a 'protestant' way of making every Christian a very strange type of Levitical priest.

Thus, a great doctrine has been perverted in the interests of a purely individualistic conception of Christian life. None of us would have come to believe the gospel had not somebody 'told' us; so, too, each of us is in debt to many who have helped to bring God to us and us to God. It is pride, not truly Protestant conviction, that causes us to forget our debt; and because we forget our debt, we fail to recognize our responsibility for each other.

This lengthy discussion of doctrine may have seemed a strange

[4] Op. cit., p. 94.

introduction to a chapter which set out to deal with practical matters, but this is just another example of the relation between theology and practice. So long as laymen seek to establish their 'equality' or identity with ministers, they fail to recognize what it means to be laymen; the more we attempt to understand an allegedly individual priesthood, the less can we appreciate the ministry of the Church as a whole.

The Church is 'a holy priesthood'; individual members share in that ministry, not (I believe) because of any particular office to which they may be called within the Church, but wholly by reason of their membership of it. In its corporate self-offering, in worship and intercession, in the sacrament of the Lord's Supper and in its total life the Church is empowered by the Spirit to offer a 'sacrifice of praise and thanksgiving', yet only and always in and through 'the one, perfect and sufficient Sacrifice'.

The whole Church shares in the whole mission of the Church. I find the most rewarding part of Kraemer's book to be his discussion of the New Testament term *diakonia* (ministry). This word, which originally described the humble service of a waiter at table, is one which Jesus made 'the typical expression for the spirit and relationships within the community of His disciples'.[5] As we follow the use of this term by New Testament writers, we find that, in Kraemer's memorable words, 'the Church *is* ministry' (*diakonia*). The Church, like her master, is to be among men as one who serves. That service is to characterize its corporate life, as well as the lives of its individual members; the Church itself is to share in the ministry of the Suffering Servant. It is by its costly love for people that the Church may prove itself to *be* the Church.

And so the pastoral ministry of the Church is fulfilled in all manner of humble service of those outside as well as of those within. Imagination and fact-finding inquiry are called for, if the Church is to render such service in a society in which the more obvious wants are being supplied; but without it the Church's teaching loses much of its power. It is, however, not accidental that, in his classification of the particular 'ministries' which Christ gives to His church, the author of Ephesians brackets together 'pastors and teachers' (Eph 4^{11}), and it is with this one teaching aspect of the pastoral office that we are here specially concerned.

[5] Op. cit., pp. 138f.

The Church is obviously engaged in a teaching ministry when individual members offer instruction to others, but the corporate teaching activity of the Church is, perhaps, less readily recognized. It takes place in at least two ways. Firstly, the Church teaches by *living* the doctrine. I have more than once commented upon the fact that Christian truth is best learnt within a truly Christian community. This is something that everyone knows who grew up in a Christian home and spent his youth in a Church that was spiritually alive. We need constantly to examine afresh every aspect of the life of the local Church and of the denomination to which we belong. How often our doctrine of the Holy Spirit is denied by the manner in which we conduct Church business! How often our proclamation of the gospel of reconciliation is made ludicrous by our behaviour towards each other!

Secondly (and supremely), the Church teaches in and through its corporate worship. I say 'teaches', not 'may teach', because, for good or ill, every public act of worship teaches more about the real beliefs of a congregation than can be taught in any sermon.

Some of the most impressive recent developments within many different denominations, including some of the lay movements to which reference has been made, take the form of liturgical revival.[6] It is to be hoped that those Methodists and others in whom the term 'liturgy' often arouses prejudice and strong emotion will not fail to learn from what is happening among many of their fellow-Christians. No liturgy can become more fixed and traditional than the order of public worship to which many of us are accustomed in Free Churches; our freedom has become a bondage greater than that of any book. I know well how discussion about forms of worship can degenerate into bitter argument about trivialities, and how useless are the attempts to improve matters by mere imitation of other denominations; but I also have experience of the value of discussion about the meaning of worship, and about what we are doing when we engage in it. Laymen have an essential part in such discussion, for, of all the calamities to which the false kind of distinction between clergy and laity has led, the most disastrous is that which has led to passivity in worship on the part of the congregation. We all need

[6] See Alfred R. Shands's fascinating introduction to this subject, *The Liturgical Movement and the Local Church*.

to learn how to worship and we need to learn what worship alone can teach us.

Theology that does not lead to worship is both false and harmful; worship that is not grounded in the knowledge and love of God is not true worship. This is brought home to our minds with especial clarity in the sacrament of Holy Communion.

There the gospel, spoken in word and in action, calls forth from the united worshippers their common Eucharist (thanksgiving) and their common service (*leitourgia*); there 'the comfortable words' are applied by the Holy Spirit Himself; there the Lord who spake gives to men the Word which is Himself. 'By this food our souls are fed'; and, as once the disciples served others with the loaves that the Lord had blessed, so every sharer in this sacrament participates in the pastoral Ministry and the Presence of the Good Shepherd.

II. 'LAY' PASTORS

Something more must now be said about the specific function of the laity in the cure of souls.[7] Revival of interest in the theology of the laity, and widespread desire for full association between ordained and lay members of Christ's Church, must not be allowed to blur the laity's distinctiveness. Alfred R. Shands has written thus about the 'lay priesthood':

It is essential to the mission [of the Church] to have a priesthood which is grounded in the life of the world. Without this great emphasis on humanity and the world, there is no priesthood. It was only through the Incarnation that Christ became priest. . . . Because the layman lives so completely in the midst of the world, at every turning he has opportunities to be a priest among men. The field of his priesthood is his 'world', all that his life touches. Because each layman lives in a different 'world', he alone can offer the gift of himself to this 'world' as an offering to God. The minister cannot do this in the same deep sense that a layman can.[8]

These words provide a fine description of what is the supreme

---

[7] I am not here using the term 'lay pastors' with the technical meaning that it sometimes bears. The Methodist Church has been nobly served by devoted men who have borne this name, but it has now been recognized (in England) that the title was ill-chosen and theologically confusing. One of its disadvantages was that it tended to conceal the pastoral nature of other offices in the Church, e.g. those of class-leader, Sunday school teacher and lay preacher.

[8] *The Liturgical Movement and the Local Church*, p. 45.

THE MINISTRY OF THE WHOLE CHURCH 149

'office open to a layman' (to use a favourite Methodist expression); it is to be a Christian layman in the world.

Unhappily, much of our Church activity seems to be set upon removing the layman from the world. Even when the Church 'goes to the factories', it is sometimes only to isolate Christians into little, self-contained groups. With many noteworthy exceptions, it is very difficult to persuade Church members that nothing which they do in 'the Church' can make up for lack of what they need to do, and to be, in 'the world'. The minister who plays at being a layman is the last man in the world to be able to help them.

Unless the whole import of this book is misconceived, the layman in the world is greatly in need of pastoral theology. Preaching a sermon to a Christian congregation is a comparatively simple task compared with holding a conversation about Christian matters with an unbeliever in a factory or office. We only discover how difficult (and how important) theology is when we take it to the outside world. That is a fact which is often forgotten by those of us who associate theological study chiefly with the college classroom or the Church gathering. The satisfaction of this lay need for pastoral theology must fall primarily upon ordained minsters (see the next chapter), but it should not, and cannot, be wholly met by them.

There have been many distinguished lay theologians, from earliest times to our own, and especially within the Orthodox Church.[9] It is worthy of note that the theological writings which have made the greatest impact upon the British public in recent years have nearly all been by non-professional theologians; T. S. Eliot, C. S. Lewis, Dorothy Sayers and Charles Williams, to mention only a few. All who desire the growth of Christ's Kingdom will recognize the need for theologically informed men and women who are also scientists, philosophers, sociologists, or creative artists. There must be no restrictive practices in theological industry.

There is no need for me to enlarge upon the services that are being given by lay preachers, lay readers, teachers in day and

[9] See Kraemer's interesting discussion of the Russian term *sobornost* and the Russian Orthodox Church's insistence upon the fulness (*pleroma*) of the whole Church—laymen and clergy. Kraemer suggests that this emphasis is unfortunately accompanied by a tendency for the thought of that Church to be directed to its own past, rather than to the world (op. cit., pp. 96ff).

Sunday schools, leaders of Bible classes, and so on. About the responsibility of professional theologians towards this large army of lay 'theologians' I shall have something to say in Chapter 12 (cf. Note A), but it is, I hope, permissible to suggest here that the help which the professional most needs from the layman, fully engaged as he is in some non-ecclesiastical occupation, is precisely about the relevance of doctrine to daily living. It is always disappointing to discover that a layman's doctrine is held, as it were, in a separate compartment of his mind.

Before leaving this subject, I should like to urge that there is one other expression of the teaching-pastoral work of the Church which needs to be developed. This is the kind of theological study which takes the form of group-discussion without the assistance of a particularly expert leader. The original Methodist Class Meeting had something of this character, for the leaders were often very far from being 'experts'. The outstanding instance of great progress in contemporary British Methodism is provided by the Methodist societies in the universities. As one who spent a considerable part of his life in touch with these societies when they were emerging from small beginnings, I am convinced that some of the lessons which they can teach are not being sufficiently widely learnt.

Of course there is much to explain the success of the groups which now form the strongest part of these societies' activities. Young students like to talk; and it is much easier to achieve happy relationships in a homogeneous company than in a mixed assortment of people such as makes up a normal Church. But many of us have also seen this kind of group prosper among those who are not students; and we have sometimes seen such groups strangled at birth by a well-intentioned effort at leadership or control by a minister or some other 'expert'. I have been criticized when I have made observations of this kind at conferences of ministers and Christian workers, but I am confirmed in my opinions in an unexpected way. One of the most fruitful developments in modern psychotherapy is the practice of group-discussion by patients. It is being proved that those whose minds have become disturbed can often help each other by 'talking out' their problems, and that they can often do for each other what no professional psychiatrist could do for them. Most of us, especially when we are young, are mentally disturbed, not in the sense that we are seriously ill, but in that our emotions, our ideas and our attitudes towards life are disordered and even chaotic. We may well need many kinds of expert help, but we also need to explore ourselves in company with others.

I believe that this comparison between the success of Christian student-groups and groups of mental hospital patients is not as absurd as it may at first appear.[10] From neither group should we exclude the power of the Holy Spirit; but a group of Christians, met in Christ's Name to discover more fully His Way, has every right to expect the Spirit's illumination. If there is a minister or some other more specially trained adviser in the background, the group will, sooner or later, seek his aid; if there is a true man of God in the neighbourhood, it will want his help. But I am sure that many people, and not only the young, need to launch out upon their own in the study of the Bible, of Christian doctrine and of the Christian Way. At least they are not so likely to think that theology is 'dull' as they are when some of us expound it to them. More importantly, they may learn that way of complete commitment to each other in which the cure of souls most easily takes place.

> Help us to build each other up,
> Our little stock improve;
> Increase our faith, confirm our hope,
> And perfect us in love.

[10] Much that is said below (pp. 157ff) about 'responsive counselling' is as relevant to group-discussion as to the particular work of ministers.

CHAPTER ELEVEN

THE MINISTRY OF THE MINISTER

IF 'the Church *is* ministry', and if all Christians may share in pastoral service, it may well be asked what distinctive place the 'minister' occupies. That question is, in fact, being widely asked by Church members and by some ministers; moreover, as we noted at the outset of this book, people outside the Church have become increasingly unclear about the minister's status and function. Whilst I have no intention of expounding a full doctrine of the ordained ministry, a little must be said on this theme before we can turn to more practical questions about the minister's part in the cure of souls.

1. A PROFESSIONAL MINISTRY

Christians who believe that ordination conveys an exclusive power to administer sacraments, and those who are convinced that ordained men have a 'priesthood' which wholly distinguishes them from laymen, do not need to answer the question that I have just posed. (There are other questions which they must answer!) I write as one who holds, with firm conviction, to the 'official' doctrine of his own denomination:

Christ's Ministers in the Church are Stewards in the household of God and Shepherds of His flock. Some are called and ordained to this sole occupation and have a principal and directing part in these great duties but they hold no priesthood differing in kind from that which is common to the Lord's people and they have no exclusive title to the preaching of the gospel or the care of souls. These ministries are shared with them by others to whom also the spirit divides His gifts severally as He wills.[1]

It is along the lines of that statement (along with further explanatory clauses to which I shall refer) that Methodists (and, I believe, many other Christians) would interpret the status of the minister and, in particular, his place within the cure of souls.

[1] *The Deed of Union* of the Methodist Church of Great Britain, Clause 30. Other quotations in this chapter are from the same source, unless otherwise stated.

'The status of the minister': the word 'status' itself points to the ease with which we ask the wrong questions about the ministry. The dictionary definition of 'status'—'social position, rank, relation to others, relative importance'—shows how confused and unworthy our inquiry may become. Questions about 'social position, rank and relative importance' have no rightful place in the minds of the followers of Him who said, 'their great men exercise authority over them. But it shall not be so among you; but whoever would be great among you must be your servant, and whoever would be first among you must be slave of all' (Mk 10^{42}). If, however, by 'status' we mean 'relation to others', then it is these words of Christ's which tell us what it must be.

The Methodist doctrinal standards, from which I have quoted, are quite wrongly understood if they are assumed to give a mainly negative account of ordination. Attention is easily focused upon the negative clauses: 'no priesthood differing in kind' . . . 'no exclusive title', etc. Let us set down the positive affirmations. Ministers are;

(a) Called of God. This 'call' is part of the call upon which the existence of the whole Church depends, but it is a particular call within that divine election. 'The office of the Christian ministry depends upon the call of God who bestows the gifts of the Spirit, the grace and the fruit which indicate those whom He has chosen'.

(b) Recognized by the Church, as those whom God has called to this ministry, and 'set apart by ordination to the Ministry of the Word and Sacraments'.

(c) Given 'a principal and directing part in these great duties', i.e., as the context shows, stewardship and shepherding.

If there are those who seek a higher status than this, or a more precise function, I am not among their number. Let it never be forgotten, moreover, that just as it is God who calls and the Church which acknowledges His call, so it is Christ Himself who ordains and the Holy Spirit who empowers, whilst the Church prays that this may happen.

Ministers have a 'principal and directing part' as shepherds of His flock; that is the one point with which the remainder of this chapter is concerned.

This implies a *professional* ministry. I use the term 'professional', well aware that many people would say, 'The one thing that we do not want is a professional ministry'. As the term 'charity' has now become an ugly word ('I don't want charity!') because it can be applied to gifts which are made without understanding and love, so the word 'professional' has fallen into disrepute because it can denote work done without devotion and enthusiasm. Its proper meaning, however, is 'belonging to a profession', or being an expert; its secondary use is to describe those who are paid as distinct from those who are 'amateurs'—or, in the peculiar language of cricket, the Players rather than the Gentlemen!

Take the secondary meaning first. We are greatly in error, I believe, if we gloss over the fact that the ministry is a 'paid profession'. A title for Methodist ministers, once common, now somewhat in disrepute, was, 'separated ministers'; it is worth preserving. Ministers *are* separated from many of the duties that fall upon those who must 'earn a living' in the world. It should not be forgotten that the ministry (in this sense) will only continue as long as the laity believe that it should be supported. The very existence of this kind of ministry is imperilled if ministers are so badly paid that, for their families' sake, they must seek supplementary income, or if, in the desire for minor luxuries, their ministry becomes less than full-time.[2]

I do not apologize for this reference to a paid ministry, for the matter of payment is also bound up with the primary meaning of 'professional': belonging to a particular profession. It would at first appear that the minister cannot be a professional in this sense, for all his 'ministries are shared by others'. But the fact that all the Lord's people are to be prophets need not prevent us from speaking about a prophetic ministry, nor does the truth that all are to be 'ministers' (servants) make it nonsensical to speak of 'the minister'. The minister is a representative minister. He is called by God, commissioned by the Church, and privileged by the circumstances of his life to be a specialist in what is the business of every Christian.

He is also selected and given training, because the Church believes that there is need for those who will exercise 'special

---

[2] I cannot myself see how a 'part-time ministry' is reconcilable with Methodist doctrine. We are now able to authorize 'lay' persons to administer the sacraments and to fulfil other 'ministerial' duties. But this matter is under review by the British Methodist Conference and another opinion may prevail, especially in respect of Overseas work.

qualifications for the discharge of special duties'. He is expected to be an expert. There is no escape from this awesome truth; he is to be an expert in knowledge of God and in the Christian ministry. That is why he is given 'a principal and directing part in these great duties' in which every Christian, according to his opportunity, must share.

We often express our regret that the quality of a local Church's life depends to such a great extent upon the quality of its minister. I do not think that we should either deny or deplore this. Every minister knows how greatly his own spiritual life depends upon the prayers, the guidance and the practical help of those to whom he ministers; and nobody imagines that ministers are always to be numbered among the most 'saintly' members of the Church. Yet God means them to be such. The vulgar nickname for a minister which was once current, 'Holy Joe', was a designation more to be coveted than many high-sounding ecclesiastical titles.

In England (whatever may be true elsewhere) Christian ministers have to win their way back into public recognition. Many of us are aware of this, and some of us are tempted to speed that task by seeking some kind of prestige or 'status'. Were we to succeed in this, we should have failed in our real purpose. When men and women discover that a minister lives in close touch with God, is able to help them to love God, cares for them with something of the care of Jesus, and ministers to them in holy things, they do not find it very difficult to think of him as '*the* minister'. It is, of course, true that God's grace can reach men through most unworthy human instruments; but that is not the whole truth, nor is it a truth upon which we should ever presume.

So far as the particular pastoral office is concerned, the implications of what has just been said are many and fairly obvious. The minister is to be a *pastor pastorum* (a shepherd of shepherds). However hard he tries, he can never be in as close and intimate contact with people far outside the Churches as can lay people. This truth is becoming increasingly appreciated in regard to evangelism, and many experiments are taking place in which ministers are helping lay folk to be evangelists. We need to extend our understanding of evangelism to include all manner of pastoral contacts. Church members are daily meeting people who are facing all kinds of difficulty, asking all manner of questions, struggling with moral temptation and seeking to find solutions to problems in their own life and that of mankind as a whole. Ministers who are helping them to meet these opportunities are, indeed, serving 'the world'. We need to re-assess the whole of our ministerial activity in order that we may concentrate upon this task. We often waste our emotions in regretting that our vocation separates us from the world, when we could be spending our energy in helping those who have every opportunity to shepherd Christ's 'other sheep'.

Those whose responsibility it is to help other shepherds must fulfil this duty whilst themselves busy in caring for the sheep. It is noteworthy that whenever one comes across a minister whose own pastoral ministry is outstanding, one finds that his people are themselves caring for others. Nothing is more infectious than Christian love. From ministers of this sort we can learn very much, and a few comments upon the lessons that some of them have taught me may not be out of place.

Our preaching must be from pastoral care to pastoral need—that it is to say, our sermons must spring out of and be directed to the needs of those whom we know and care for. Obvious as this necessity may appear, every preacher knows how easily he can forget it. Yet our preaching must be determined not by our pastoral experience, but by the gospel, or else we shall follow, rather than lead, the flock.

In our personal contacts, in 'visiting' and in consultations, we must seek to be true professionals. People do not really want to see us because we are 'just like everybody else'; they need us (and many of them consciously want us) because we are different from most people. They know why they want the doctor, they understand the purpose of the rate-collector's visit, and, deep in their hearts, they know why the minister calls, or why they call to see him. Often when they most determinedly make it difficult for us to talk about God, this is because they so greatly need us to do so; if we did not find it so difficult to do this, they would be less afraid.

If these remarks appear to be censorious, I trust that the reader will understand that I make them, not only out of experience of personal failure, but also from observation of ministerial brethren who are fulfilling this ministry, sometimes under most adverse conditions. It is a ministry from which we may well shrink. Even the intellectual demands made upon those who would teach others to teach are great, but the cost of being shepherds who both care for the sheep and shepherd other shepherds is much greater. Some words written about pastors by John Wesley are worth quoting:

> They are supposed to go before the flock (as is the manner of the eastern shepherds to this day), and to guide them in all the ways of truth and holiness; they are to 'nourish them with the words of eternal life'; to feed them with the 'pure milk of the word': applying it continually 'for doctrine', teaching them all the essential doctrines contained therein; 'for reproof'... 'for correction'... and 'for instruction in righteousness'; training them up to outward holiness....
> 'They watch', waking while others sleep, over the flock of Christ.... They have them in their hearts both by day and by night; regarding neither sleep nor food in comparison of them. Even while they sleep, their heart is waking, full of concern for their beloved children.[3]

Even that is but a little for us to do for the Good Shepherd, who laid down His life for the sheep.

II. SPIRITUAL DIRECTION AND RESPONSIVE COUNSELLING

I turn now to a matter which is arousing considerable attention among students and practitioners of pastoral counselling, and about which much more has been written in North America than in England. The traditional term 'spiritual direction' is in ill-favour with many (see p. 20, above). The objection is not directed against the minister as such, but against the whole notion of direction.

The distaste for direction has two causes which are related to each other. On the one hand, it is argued that any kind of moral judgement should be avoided by the pastor; on the other hand, it is said to be wrong for any personal interview to involve explicit direction. The former objection is mainly ethical and the latter is primarily psychological; there is much to be said for each of them.

I shall not repeat what I have previously said about our moral judgements upon other people (pp. 113ff). It is, however, very important that refusal to assess the moral culpability of someone who has sought our help should not result in our giving an appearance of moral indifference. People would not consult us about

[3] John Wesley, Sermon 97, *On Obedience to Pastors*.

their personal morality unless they believed that we could help them to discover what is right and good. Except in the instance of those who are so mentally sick that they cannot themselves form moral judgements, a Christian minister should never (I believe) conceal his own moral convictions, although he should always seek to show that they are grounded in Christian truth, rather than in personal prejudice or conventional moral notions.

The strength of the objection to ethical direction lies in the grounds for dislike of direction of any kind. Many writers make a sharp distinction between 'directive' and 'non-directive' counselling. Paul E. Johnson has well defined these terms as follows. 'A directive counsellor', he writes, 'takes control of the interview by asking leading questions to conduct his own investigation along the lines of his interest and gain the information he considers most important.' He makes his diagnosis, selects 'the goals that the person has been unable to choose for himself', and then explicitly directs his path, resisting (or attempting to resist) all obstacles set up by the inquirer. 'A non-directive counsellor places responsibility upon the person to lead the conversation according to his interests, tell what he is ready to admit, discover his own insights, choose his own goals, and decide what steps he will take in working towards them.'[4]

As a description of wrong and right ways of counselling this requires no criticism. But as Johnson points out, 'non-directive' is a misnomer for the second type of counselling. 'There must be subtle guidance in every step. . . . The counsellor is not in a passive rôle. . . . Without . . . selective and confirming activity by the counsellor progress is unlikely to occur.' Johnson therefore proposes the term *responsive counselling* as a more accurate designation of what the pastoral counsellor aims at. I believe this to be a valuable corrective to much muddled thought about 'non-directive' counselling, and I would venture to commend Johnson's most practical book, especially to young ministers.

This same matter has been discussed by Donald D. Evans in an article which I have previously mentioned.[5] He remarks that the objection to moral judgement by the counsellor is often expressed as a positive demand for 'acceptance' by the counsellor.

---

[4] Paul E. Johnson, *Pastoral Ministration*, pp. 78f.
[5] 'Pastoral Counselling and Traditional Theology', *Scottish Journal of Theology*, XI.2, pp. 172ff; see p. 47, above.

That is to say, the counsellor must never show any moral disapproval; he must 'accept' the ethical situation. Evans rightly suggests that in so far as this is a way of describing the kind of loving sympathy which never turns away from any sinner, it is a basic requirement of the Christian pastor. But he also shows how unsatisfactory the 'acceptance' principle is if it is applied to all situations.

Evans goes a long way towards agreement with the idea of non-direction, but he adds important qualifications. I quote a few of his words:

Where a person is in a situation of psychological threat and accepts only those interpretations which enable him to evade his real problem, it is usually useless and sometimes dangerous to present Christian doctrine. Non-directive therapy may help him to gain the self-knowledge which leads to mental health and maturity; pastors may use it as part of their ministry of healing in such cases. When this stage is reached, there is a place for rational discussion or persuasion concerning doctrine.

This is a very balanced statement. The pastor's most difficult decision is to know when to speak and when to keep silent, when to lead and when to refrain from leading. We are, I think, only just beginning to study the art of spiritual direction in some of our theological colleges, but even if we were giving better instruction to future ministers, every pastor (ministerial or lay) must learn in the school of experience. It is a pity that we so rarely keep private records of our interviews, and so fail to learn from our failures and successes.

There is, however, one way in which we may all learn about these matters; it is from Jesus Christ Himself. The term 'responsive counselling' is not an unworthy one to apply to Him.

Jesus refused to rescue men and women from the responsibility of personal thought, decision and action. He, who knew all things about God, asked them, 'What do *you* think?' Upon people who were bewildered by all kinds of false prophets He laid the responsibility of decision about a new prophetic command: 'But I say unto you . . .'. He set men asking questions, and He answered question with question. Above all, He allowed those whom He loved, even those who also loved Him, to make their own mistakes, to commit their own sins, to reject Him if they would. His Church has always found it hard to follow in His steps.

But Jesus was by no means a 'non-directive' counsellor. He never blurred moral issues in the interests of sentimental kindness; He left men in no doubt about what He knew to be the truth; He taught in plain language, but He taught explicitly and categorically. If Paul was afraid to give strong meat to babes, Jesus gave thanks to His Father that things hidden from the wise and understanding had been revealed to infants.

A pastor will not be short of an exemplar, nor will he be tempted to covet the role of a psychotherapist, if he thinks of his work as that of following in the footsteps of Jesus the Shepherd. But we are not like Him; we can only, slowly, humbly and painfully, learn from Him. Therefore we must yet again recall that it is God the Holy Spirit who is the true Counsellor. As Paul Johnson has finely said, 'A directive counsellor may vest authority in himself as the healer. A non-directive counsellor may vest authority in the person as one who solves his own problems. A pastoral counsellor will vest authority in the creative Holy Spirit working in both through a relationship that is not a dualism of counsellor and person, but a trinity of Creator, person, and counsellor.'[6]

Whilst, then, it is natural, and on occasion fitting, that ordained and lay people alike should ask, 'What is a minister?' that is never the question of chief importance. The more closely the clergy are associated with the laity, the more fully will both discover what are their proper place and function within the ministry which is Christ's gift to the Church. We need a holy rivalry between the parson and the layman; but neither can be jealous to preserve his own prerogatives or territory; neither exists for himself; both exist for Christ and for all for whom Christ died. There is only one 'place' for the shepherd, and that is among the sheep.

[6] Op. cit., p. 81.

CHAPTER TWELVE

THE MINISTRY OF THE THEOLOGIAN[1]

BY 'theologians' I mean, in this chapter, those who are specially engaged upon the study of one or more of the many branches of theological inquiry. It is much less easy to define the meaning of 'theology', whether as used in this chapter or anywhere else. The reader must have observed to himself, on many occasions when this word has been used in preceding pages: 'It all depends upon what he means by "theology".' P. T. Forsyth once attempted to describe two kinds of theology thus:

> There is theology and 'theology'. There is the theology which is a part of the Word, and the theology which is a product of it. There is a theology which is sacramental and is the body of Christ, so to say; and there is a theology which is but scientific and descriptive and memorial. There is a theology which quickens, and one which elucidates. There is a theology which is valuable because it is evangelical, and one which is valuable because it is scholastic. It is no Christianity which cannot say: 'I believe in God the Creator who, in Christ, is my Almighty Father, Judge and Redeemer.' That is theology, but not 'theology'.... But our laity has not yet learned to distinguish between these two senses of Christian truth.[2]

I must not stay to discuss Forsyth's charge that 'the Reformation succumbed to a theological hierarchy instead of a sacerdotal', or his opinions that the laity are 'victims to an anachronistic suspicion of an obsolete "theology"', and that we are in danger of relapsing 'to that dogmatocracy, that rule of the professional theologian' which (he held) was one aspect of seventeenth-century Protestantism. There is much in this passage which is debatable, and half a century has passed since it was written, yet there is much in it which speaks to our condition.

Firstly, Forsyth, in making his distinction between theology and 'theology', affirmed the value of both. There is much theology

---

[1] Readers who are not interested in the technicalities of theological study may prefer to pass on to the closing chapter. If they do so, it will be, I hope, because they are not interested in what I have written, not because they are uninterested in the work of theologians.
[2] P. T. Forsyth, *The Person and Place of Jesus Christ* (5th Ed.), pp. 15f.

which is valuable, even necessary, which is not essential to Christian living. It seems to me that theologians could give greater help in this connexion than most of them do. Which parts of the inquiry, and which results of the inquiry now being made by all kinds of theological scholars, need to be made known to the non-specialist? I have named a few examples of theological writers whose works perform this very task, and many more could have been given; but I believe that one of the first tasks of the ecumenical study of theology, which is now developing, should be in this field.[3]

I should like to use an analogy from the medical profession, although the comparison cannot be exact. Some of those who are engaged in medical research may be too busily occupied to ask which details of their research, and which results of their experiments, should be made known to the general public, and how quickly this should be done; but somebody must decide, otherwise rumour and ill-founded hopes will cause injury, and much-needed remedies will not be sought. Those who are engaged upon the study of sacred learning have an even greater responsibility towards 'the public'. Again, in medicine the general practitioner has a very important part to play in this selection and transmission of medical knowledge. The old type of physician, who often concealed facts from his patient, even if he did not deliberately deceive him, and who was content to prescribe a 'bottle' without any account of what the drug was intended to do, has given place to the doctor who seeks to help his patients to understand the nature both of their sickness and of the steps being taken towards their cure.

The local minister or parish clergyman may be described as the general practitioner. Or, to change the comparison, he may be likened to the middle-man between the theologians and the people. A great many very practical matters are suggested by this conception of the minister's function. I think of the inability of most ministers to purchase books, and of the physical remoteness of many from the centres of learning—both facts which make it difficult for them to keep in touch with theological scholarship. I might also refer to ministerial overwork, were it not that the busiest ministers known to me are also among the ones who read most books. More serious is the lack, in this country, of theological

[3] See Note A, p. 167.

journals which adequately meet the needs of those who, although they have 'studied theology', would not describe themselves as theologians.[4] These and other difficulties are actual and serious, but they cannot be allowed to prevent the discharge of this kind of pastoral duty, which includes both a teaching ministry and a work of liaison between the laity and the theologians.

The general practitioner, in his turn, depends upon the specialist if he is to fulfil his own duties. It must be difficult for those whose gifts and talents call them to complete concentration upon their studies and professional teaching to find time to communicate more widely, by speech and writing, the fruits of their work; we must be very grateful to those who do this. But this co-operation between theologians and ministers in pastoral work will only develop when we all recognize more widely the needs of the laity.

This leads to a further point suggested by the quotation from Forsyth, which is underlined elsewhere in the same book. He affirmed that there was danger of relapse into 'the rule of the professional theologian'. I do not see any strong evidence (at least, not in Churches with which I am most familiar) of any widespread domination by theologians; there is, however, not a little fear of them, often jocularly expressed, but none the less real. Even more common is the assumption that theology (in all senses of the word) belongs to the theologians. It is perhaps worth trying to see, a little more clearly, how and why this situation has arisen. I will mention only three contributory factors.

First, we have not yet recovered from the destructive effects of the theological movement which is commonly described as 'liberal-protestant' (though it should not be forgotten that we are also benefiting by some positive results of that movement). Very many people, and by no means only the little-educated, are suspicious that the theologian is hard at work destroying the beliefs of 'ordinary' Christians. It is little wonder that this thought is current, for most people have had little opportunity to learn about the revival of biblical theology, the positive achievements of biblical criticism, or the general 'revival of theology' about which theologians delight to speak to each other.

[4] I am not unmindful of help that is provided by a number of magazines, but I have in mind an English counterpart to the American *Theology Today*.

In the second place, theological scholarship has itself become more complex. I mean, not that theologians of past centuries were less competent, nor that their work was less scholarly, but that the growth of the use of certain scientific methods by theologians, the multiplication of the divisions and sub-divisions into which their work is now separated, and (perhaps most significantly of all) the most desirable increase of theological discussion across denominational frontiers—all these and other changes have made theology a highly complex discipline. One result of this is that theologians themselves share with other modern students the perils of extreme specialization; another result is that it has become almost impossible for those who are outside the little world of the specialists to see the wood for the trees.

The third contributory cause of the increasing tendency to leave theology to the specialists is a by-product of one of the most promising characteristics of contemporary theological scholarship—namely, the revival of biblical theology.

I use the phrase 'revival of biblical theology' because it is commonly employed, but it might well be argued that we have witnessed, during the last fifty years, not merely a revival but a fresh discovery of biblical theology. This has been one of the positive gains to which the apparently purely destructive 'liberal' period contributed. It is not surprising that voices are being raised in criticism of this biblical theology itself; thought proceeds by criticism and counter-criticism, and the easiest way to write a book is to centre it upon the errors of other writers. We should not be intimidated by those who use 'neo-fundamentalism' and 'neo-orthodoxy' as terms of abuse; but there is a danger in the present concentrated study of the scriptures, as there is always peril in any worthwhile effort.

The danger is that those who consider the main task of theology to be that of understanding the Bible should stop short of the further task of interpreting the Bible. If 'liberals' forsook the Bible in order to interpret the gospel 'in modern terms', and if extreme 'conservatives' escape from the responsibility of understanding the Bible by treating it as though it were a divinely constructed gramophone disc to be passively 'heard', there is yet another false way; it is that of resting content with finding out what the Bible says without asking what it means.

That the Bible is its own best interpreter, that there is *a* theology of the Bible (and not merely many 'theologies' in the Bible), and that a host of contributory studies—textual, archaeological, linguistic, literary, etc.—can help us to understand the Bible better than it has ever been understood, these (I believe) are true and important facts, and yet it is possible to discover precisely what the Bible says without discovering what the Bible means to us.

I do not want to deny that some specialists must stand aside from the task of communicating the thought of the Bible to the non-intellectual. Neither am I suggesting that we should make the mistake, once again, of thinking that Christian truth can be conveyed by words which are entirely different from those in which it was first expressed, or fall into the error of assuming that the purpose of a Christian thinker is to extract from the Bible such items as appear to be in harmony with current thought. Many very stupid things have been said about 'the problem of communication' based on assumptions such as these. What I am trying to do is to echo, however faintly, the words of Jesus: 'You search the scriptures, because you think that in them you have eternal life; and it is they that bear witness to me' (Jn 5^{39}).

We do not have to be 'fundamentalists' to incur that rebuke. Perhaps we can best see what needs to be avoided by considering those theological scholars who provide us with an example of the right approach. (It would be invidious to mention names, but names will doubtless occur to any student.) When, in some work of highly technical theological scholarship, we hear the note of adoring wonder, or when (for example) a discussion of eschatology confronts us with the judgement and the mercy of Christ, or when a detailed examination of the literary structure of a minor prophet helps us to hear for ourselves the prophetic word, or when (to adapt words of Edwyn Hoskyns) we encounter scholars who have buried themselves in a lexicon and risen in the presence of God, then we begin to learn what the Bible *means*.

All of us whom the church has bidden to spend our days in the study and teaching of theology know how grave is the danger in which we have been set. Perhaps no human task is more spiritually perilous than this. We must never lose sight of the fact that Christian doctrine is for life, for the life of Everyman. That is why I have devoted this space to comment upon Forsyth's appeal that theology should never be taken away from the layman. What he wrote about the particular doctrine of Christology may be applied to the whole of Christian belief:

> All Christology exists in the interest of the evangelical faith of the layman who has in Jesus Christ the pardon of his sins and everlasting life. We are all laymen here. It is quite misplaced patronage to condescend to lay experience with the superiority of the academic theologian or the idealist philosopher, and to treat such lay experience of the Gospel as if it were good enough for most, and the only one they are yet fit for, but if they passed through the schools they would be able to put their belief on another and better footing.[5]

Do we need to add to all the many branches of theology a specialized study of pastoral theology? (So far as I can gather, most theological college courses on 'pastoral theology'—outside Roman Catholic seminaries—tend to deal primarily with pastoral techniques, and with other practical aspects of the work of the ministry.) There may be convenience in the separation of pastoral from other types of theological study, but I think that by too complete isolation the loss would be greater than the gain; for then the expert in historical theology might be tempted to conceal the fact that he is studying the thought of real people in actual Church- and life-settings, the professor of biblical studies might lead his students to think that the Epistles had been properly studied when they had remembered theories about the authorship of Ephesians and ignored the gospel in Ephesians, and the lecturer in systematic theology (or dogmatics) might, even more calamitously, fail to show what his subject is really about. There is, I hope, room for special study of the pastoral character of Christian doctrine (if not, this slight introduction to that subject has been badly misconceived), but let us beware of increased departmentalizing.

I must conclude this chapter by turning attention yet once more, to the attitude toward theology of the non-theologian. The fault in the present situation is not all on one side. On the part of many people, both within and outside the Church, there is a foolish readiness to assume that any man can manufacture his own theology. The questions that are asked (to which I have several times made reference) do not always manifest a humble desire to

[5] Op. cit., p. 9.

learn; people who, in other spheres of human knowledge, readily look to the expert do not even trouble to learn what theological experts say, before they criticize and pronounce judgement. There are displays of this attitude by well-known people, in print and in broadcasting, which can rightly be described as impertinent. Even within the Churches—sometimes especially there—there is eagerness to hear what is already believed rather than what is true.

Denunciation of such failings will not have much effect; mutual recriminations between teachers and taught will only aggravate the situation. Nobody can ever learn anything until he wants to learn it, and a teacher can never do more than help others to teach themselves, although he may make it easier or harder for them to do this. So far as the human share in the theological aspect of the cure of souls is concerned, those who speak must be content to speak the truth in love; they cannot command hearing ears and receptive minds. But if the theology that is taught is in fact a word about God, however faint and limited that word is, it can be a means through which God Himself comes to men; as Forsyth said, theology can be sacramental.

Were it not so, there would be little meaning in the term 'pastoral theology'. In the providence of God, theological study and theological instruction have their healing work to do within the cure of souls. All who share in that ministry do well to be mindful of their partners. Scholars making researches in a score of different fields of study, parents and teachers telling little children about their heavenly Father, small companies of Christian people exploring together the truth that is in Christ Jesus, individual pastors, men and women, ordained and lay, counselling others in the things that belong to God, and those who whisper the 'comforting words' to the sick and the dying— these, and many more, are pastor-teachers of the flock of Christ.

Note A

FUNDAMENTAL DOCTRINES

The plea (made on p. 162) that theologians should assist the Church by distinguishing the doctrines which are most essential to full Christian life is a request which I hope may receive serious consideration. In *The Rule of Faith* (a book which maintains its usefulness after half a century), W. P. Paterson provided (in Appendix I) a most valuable historical and critical study of 'the distinction between fundamental and non-fundamental doctrines'.

He showed how greatly this distinction was emphasized in the seventeenth century by Lutheran and Reformed theologians. Both based the fundamental distinction upon the bearing of doctrines upon individual salvation, although there were significant divergences in their classification. Hooker accepted the same kind of distinction, and many Anglican theologians of the eighteenth century wrote about this theme, from points of view which are of much interest to the student of historical theology.

This attempt to differentiate fundamental from non-fundamental doctrines may readily be confused with two other ways of dividing doctrines into classes. Firstly, there is the distinction which has often been made between 'natural' and 'revealed' theology. This method of separating 'truths of reason' from 'revealed truths' is not a method which I wish to advocate. Secondly, there is the distinction, characteristic of Roman theology, by which some truths are declared to be obligatory (to be accepted *de fide*) whilst others are treated as matters for opinion and discussion, at least by the recognized teachers of the church.

This is a question which raises many difficult problems which lie outside my scope here, but what I have in mind is something very different from either of the distinctions mentioned in the previous paragraph. There are (I believe) doctrines which are essential to the fulness of Christian belief and Christian living; and there are ways of understanding many of those doctrines which win the common consent of very many Christians today. On the other hand, there are matters of theological importance which belong, rather, to the periphery of Christian thought, and there are also matters about which there is no common Christian agreement. It is for the making of *this* kind of distinction that I ask. If the task is to be attempted afresh, certain dangers must be avoided and certain positive steps taken.

The main dangers are these. (1) There is the risk of making the concept of Christian life (the idea of salvation) too narrow. 'Evangelicals', for example, have sometimes worked with so narrow a conception of salvation that their 'fundamental doctrines' have been unhelpfully restricted. (2) There is the hazard of defining 'fundamental' in a party or sectarian spirit. (3) There is the great danger, if this distinction is made, that we should treat the 'non-fundamental' doctrines as though they were unimportant. This is particularly so when it is the difficulty of understanding the doctrine, rather than its intrinsic value, which is the point at issue. For example, I do not see how it is possible, in the present state of New Testament scholarship, for exact beliefs to be affirmed about our Lord's teaching concerning the consummation of the Age; but should this mean that no teaching about the Last Things should be given? I think not.

The positive necessities would seem to be as follows. (1) For this task there is supreme need for a theology which is ecumenical. At the moment the evidence for a surprisingly large measure of doctrinal agreement among Christians of all the major denominations, and of disagreement running right across (not between) denominational frontiers, is known only by the few who attend theological conferences and read each other's books. The Church as a whole is quite unaware of all this. (2) Each denomination has, I suggest, particular responsibility to help its members to know what are the beliefs which its theological leaders consider to be most important. In the present divided state of Christendom, this can usually only be done by each denomination separately (see Note B). (3) The interpretation of 'fundamental doctrines' must not be determined by ephemeral considerations. In each generation, specific individual and social needs draw attention to particular Christian doctrines, and it is precisely because those who are most actively engaged in pastoral work are inclined to be wholly absorbed in these more obviously needed doctrines, that those whose work makes them more detached from the pressure of immediate 'problems' must be concerned with the fulness of the Christian Faith.

Finally, it may be useful to quote Paterson's own summary of the fundamental doctrines. He says that they must include at least—

(a) a list of the blessings of the Christian religion; (b) the Christian doctrine of God—revealed as Father, Son and Holy Ghost; and (c) a statement of the gracious conditions on which man enjoys forgiveness and has the promise of eternal life, and of the consequent aspirations and obligations of the Christian calling.[1]

[1] Op. cit., p. 428.

Note B

METHODIST DOCTRINE

I increasingly discover that members of other Christian denominations ask what Methodists mean when they speak about 'Methodist doctrine'; it is also not unusual to meet Methodists who are ill-informed on this matter, or who believe that Methodist doctrinal standards are vague and indefinite. It may, therefore, be of interest to some readers if a note is added about this. Comments made upon the facts are my own, and they carry no official authority.

The doctrinal standards of the (British) Methodist Church are laid down in the *Deed of Union*, which was adopted by the Uniting Conference by the powers given to it in the Methodist Church Union Act of 1929. Clause 30, which sets forth these standards, is explicitly stated to be unalterable by the Methodist Conference; but that Conference is established as the final authority, within the Methodist Church, with regard to all questions concerning the *interpretation* of these doctrines. The following quotations from Clause 30 are most essential to the understanding of Methodist doctrine:

The Methodist Church claims and cherishes its place in the Holy Catholic Church which is the Body of Christ. It rejoices in the inheritance of the Apostolic Faith and loyally accepts the fundamental principles of the historic creeds and of the Protestant Reformation. It ever remembers that in the Providence of God Methodism was raised up to spread Scriptural Holiness through the land by the proclamation of the Evangelical Faith and declares its unfaltering resolve to be true to the Divinely appointed mission.

The Doctrines of the Evangelical Faith which Methodism has held from the beginning and still holds are based upon the Divine revelation recorded in Holy Scriptures. The Methodist Church acknowledges this revelation as the supreme rule of faith and practice.

Further reference is then made to the 'Evangelical Doctrines', and three things are made plain: (1) they are contained in Wesley's *Notes on the New Testament* and the first four volumes of his *Sermons;* (2) all Methodist Preachers are pledged to these doctrines; and (3) the *Notes* and *Sermons* are not to impose 'a system of formal or speculative theology on Methodist Preachers, but to set up standards of preaching and belief which secure loyalty to the fundamental truths of the Gospel of Redemption and ensure the continued witness of the Church to the realities of the Christian experience of salvation'.

I should like to make the following comments:

(1) The order of priority in these standards is of the utmost importance. The order is:

   (i) The Bible.
   (ii) Fundamental principles of Creeds and Reformation.
   (iii) Evangelical Doctrines (as in Wesley's writings).

It is explicitly and repeatedly made clear that the Bible is the sole foundation and 'the supreme rule'. Items (ii) and (iii) are included in the standards precisely because they are believed to be true and necessary comments upon the Divine revelation recorded in the Bible. We treasure these because they help us to hold the Apostolic Faith.

(2) We entirely misrepresent Methodist doctrinal standards if we emphasize (iii) in such a way as to minimize either (ii) or (i). The 'Evangelical Doctrines' referred to in the Deed are commonly described as 'Methodist emphases'. I am not aware that these have even been authoritatively defined with more precision than is suggested by the quotations already given, but I think that all Methodists would agree that they include the following doctrines: Justification by faith, assurance, Christian perfection. I trust that, however briefly and inadequately, I have indicated, in earlier parts of this book, my own sympathy with these 'emphases'; I wish now to make somewhat critical comments upon possible misunderstanding of their significance.

(*a*) It should not be thought that Methodists claim exclusive loyalty to these doctrines. To what degree any other denomination neglects any of them, and to what extent contemporary Methodists believe and teach them, are matters for objective examination. We emphasize these doctrines, not because we want to differ from other Christians, but because we believe them to be part of the Apostolic Faith.

(*b*) Any attempt to teach these particular doctrines that is not accompanied by a full presentation of the whole body of doctrine contained in the Bible and expounded in the Creeds and by the Protestant Reformers is perilous in the extreme. At several points, in earlier chapters, I sought to indicate how this mistake may be made. Something has gone amiss in Methodism when it is possible for people to hear much about 'assurance' or about 'perfect love' without receiving adequate instruction about the Person and work of the Holy Spirit. Methodist doctrinal standards are not being retained if Church members are quite unfamiliar with the Creeds, or if the celebration of 'Wesley Day' is accompanied by neglect of Trinity Sunday.

(3) The fact that the Methodist Conference is responsible for the interpretation of these standards is also important. The implication is that the Church has a continuing task of interpretation. These doctrinal standards seek to secure that such interpretation is based upon clearly defined sources, with the Bible as the ultimate and final source; they also seek to leave room for, and to make imperative, the duty of the living Church to interpret them afresh. This is part of the oversight (the *episcopé*), i.e. the pastoral care of the Church; it is laid clearly upon the Conference, and in recent years the Conference has manifested renewed devotion to this theological responsibility, as, for example, in its statement, *The Nature of the Christian Church* (1937), or in the *Statement on Holy Baptism* (1952). It is now at work upon the doctrine of Ordination.

(4) Whilst the interpretation of doctrine is the responsibility of the Conference, the duty of providing instruction is much more widely distributed. About every infant baptized in a Methodist Church the promise is made that he will be 'instructed and trained in the doctrines ... of the Christian religion'; parents, Sunday school teachers and all Church members have responsibility for the fulfilment of this pledge. Every person received into the full membership of the Methodist Church is (if properly prepared) made familiar with the doctrinal standards at which we have been looking.

It is right and proper, however, that more explicit doctrinal tests should be made of those who preach; and whenever Methodism functions properly, such tests are applied, to lay and ordained preachers. Those who are ordained to the ministry in the Methodist Church are repeatedly reminded in their ordination service of the importance of doctrine and the supremacy of Holy Scripture. They promise 'to minister *the Doctrine* and Sacraments, and the Discipline of Christ', and, when the office and work of 'a Minister and Pastor' has been committed to them, they are exhorted: 'take heed unto yourselves and to *the doctrine*'.

CHAPTER THIRTEEN

SHEPHERDS WHO ARE ALSO SHEEP

THE reader has observed, I hope, two difficulties that beset me as I wrote this book. (1) At many points I have found myself describing what we Christians need to do, whilst at the same time I have wanted to describe what we need to have done for us. At every stage in any discussion of the cure of souls, it is the same people who are physicians and patients. (2) I have found difficulty in finding a term with which to describe those who are 'patients'. Translated into the pastoral imagery, the former difficulty is due to the fact that we are all both shepherds and sheep; the latter problem is to find a suitable alternative to 'sheep', for valuable as that similitude sometimes is for some purposes, it is essential to recognize that human beings never are sheep.

A word about the latter point will lead us to further reflection upon the former. In 'catholic' writings the term 'penitent' is often used about those who receive the pastoral ministry, and—more often and perhaps more wisely—there is an unhesitating use of the word 'soul'. In 'protestant' usage there is no consistency. We often speak of 'inquirers'; but this has two disadvantages. It suggests that those in need will always seek for help, whereas the 'sheep' need to be sought; it is the shepherd who inquires for the sheep, not *vice versa*. Secondly, 'inquirers' focuses too much attention upon the question-and-answer aspect of pastoral care. In recent books on pastoral themes, we find such varied terms as 'person', 'parishioner', 'seeker' and (even!) 'client'.

At first sight, this problem about terminology seems to reflect discredit upon the pastoral office. The physician, the lawyer and the tradesman have no such difficulty in describing those whom they serve. On further reflection, however, this small verbal obstacle is a reminder of the uniqueness of the pastoral relationship. There is really only one vocabulary that suits this relationship—it is that of family relationships. Whenever we meet each other in a pastoral relationship it is as brothers and sisters; all are our brethren, whether brethren in Christ or brothers for whom also Christ died. By God's grace, any one of us may become a spiritual 'father' (or 'mother') to another human being, but it is as brethren that we meet.

We must, therefore, give to the term 'responsive counselling' a deeper meaning than was given to it in Chapter 11. Whether the pastoral relationship is between two individuals, or between one person and a group of people, or within a group in which there is no leader, there must always be this responsiveness to each other. That is no less true if the pastor is 'the minister'. Particular questions arise about the degree to which the individual pastor should speak to those whom he is seeking to help about his own needs, his own experience and his own personal faith; sensitivity and tact, as well as close dependence upon the leadings of the Holy Spirit, are needful if such questions are to be answered. But I do not believe that there is any pastoral relationship in which we must not expect to receive as well as to give.

Pastors must expect to receive from those who are being 'pastored'. It is platitudinous to say that there is no better way to learn than to teach, but that is especially true when the subject of our teaching is God. Pastoral activity, of any type, is a way of mutual enrichment. Even more essential is the expectation that we shall receive from God Himself. That divine blessing is the experience of a genuine Methodist class-meeting, or of any group of people who meet together to explore together the deep things of God; it is the humbling and unforgettable experience of any man who is privileged to help another person nearer to God.

To revert, for the last time, to the shepherd-sheep illustration, it may be said that the essence of the Church's own life lies in the fact that all are sheep who are called to share in the work of the Great Shepherd of our souls. In every part of their corporate activity, this purpose should guide the thought, and prompt the actions, of members of Christ's Church. When they worship together, they are both feeding their own souls, and helping others to feed on the Bread of life; every individual worshipper helps or hinders his fellows. When they meet together to study, to work, or to play, they meet as those who depend upon God for everything, and as those who depend upon each other in everything. And when they heal each other's wounds, it is by bringing each other to the only Healer of souls. In this receiving and giving is the rhythm of spiritual life.

But it is always from God that we receive, even though many of His gifts come to us through human hands. That is, at one and the same time, why theology has so important a part in the cure of souls and why 'theology' may be the greatest hindrance to that cure. The latter danger has never been far from our minds during the course of this book. The first commandment is not that we should become good theologians; it is that we should love God with all our powers. Emil Brunner once wrote, 'A God who is neuter makes no claims; He simply allows Himself to be looked at'[1]; but we must also remember, that, if God is to be loved by men, they must know much about Him.

The connexion between 'knowing' and 'knowing about' God occupied our attention early in this book (pp. 43ff); at its close we must return to it. Never was there so strange a commandment as this commandment to love God. Love, we might assume, is the one activity that can never be commanded. It is helpful to recall that love is more than an emotion, that it is what psychologists term a sentiment, and includes thought and activity of will, as well as feeling; even so, we are more accustomed to think of love as something that 'happens', or as something into which we 'fall', than as something that we can be commanded to do.

Moreover, to love God, whom no man has ever seen—how can that be possible? We who have heard and used these words about loving God so often, and who have, however inadequately, loved Him, are quick to forget how un-natural this love is. Fear, reverence, awe—these are descriptions of man's attitude towards the divine which natural man can comprehend, even if he does not himself believe. All the events of sacred history had to occur before a man would write, in one-syllable words: GOD IS LOVE (1 Jn 4[16]). Since then, everything that Christians have rightly said about God they have said about God who is love, and if they have loved God it has been only because 'He first loved us.'

Gustaf Aulén, in the course of a noble commentary upon the affirmation, 'God is love', writes:

> The whole exposition of the content of Christian faith is in reality the only adequate presentation of this fundamental theme. Christian faith cannot make a statement which does not in one way or another throw light on the nature of divine love.[2]

---

[1] *Man in Revolt*, p. 432.   [2] Gustaf Aulén, *The Faith of the Christian Church*, p. 133.

The proclamation of the gospel is the telling of 'the old, old story' about the way in which God manifested His love: 'God so loved . . .', 'This was the way God loved . . .'; Christian theologizing is part of the Church's continuing attempt to understand that love, that divine nature, better; Christian life is life that is lived in and by and for that love.

The cure of souls, which is only our work because it is Christ's work and because we are Christ's, is a means through which we may be brought into that love and enabled to live and grow in it. Because we are desperately sick until 'grace has touched our hearts', this cure is a work of healing; because it is the expression of love, this cure is a work of caring—God's caring for us and ours for one another. Because God is God, this cure of souls is possible; because men are men, our share in it is always imperfect. Nor must we ever forget that this life is not all. It is to the resurrection life that patients in the 'hospital' of the Church are discharged; no discharge is possible here.

So theology has its rightful place within the pastoral care of the Church when it springs from love, is about love and leads to love—love of God and of our neighbour. It has its place because we must learn about God and cannot discover Him for ourselves; it has its place because we need to increase in knowledge, until, at last, we shall no longer ask questions. 'Now we see in a mirror dimly, but then face to face. Now I know in part; then I shall understand fully, even as I have been fully understood' (1 Cor 13^{12}).

But as long as we live in this world, we must continue to look in the 'mirror', and we must tell others what we have seen. All of us who owe our own salvation to Christ have our share in the pastoral work of the Church, and upon some there is laid more heavily the task of being pastor-teachers. That responsibility, like every task that God gives to His children, is neither a reward that we have earned nor a work for which we have adequate natural powers. We can only do our work because it is His work; we can only tend the sheep because we are tended by the Lord. And so we pray for each other: 'May the God of peace who brought again from the dead our Lord Jesus, the great shepherd of the sheep, by the blood of the eternal covenant, equip you with everything good that you may do His will, working in you that which is pleasing in His sight, through Jesus Christ; to whom be the glory for ever and ever. Amen.' (Heb 13^{20f}).

INDEX

Assurance, 79ff
Augustine, 10
Aulén, G., 115n, 176

Baillie, D. M., 56, 60n, 64
Baptism, 36, 93f
Barth, K., 54, 71, 118n
Baxter, R., 11f
Bible, 33, 164f
Bonhoeffer, D., 105
Brunner, E., 176
Bucer, M., 10

Carrington, P., 14
Catechetical teaching, 10ff, 15, 36f
Cell, G. C., 70f
Church, Chaps. 6 and 10
  Denominations, 29ff, 84, 169
  Renewal, 92f
  and Social Changes, 21ff, 27ff
  and Theology, 40
  Unity, 84, 88
  Wholeness, 90, 143ff
Clergy, 143ff
Confession, 119ff
Conscience, 124f
Counselling, 18f, 157ff, 175
Creation, 102ff
Creeds, 35f
Cullmann, O., 35ff

Davies, R. E., 85
Death, 137ff
Diem, H., 42
Dillistone, F. W., 8, 89
Dodd, C. H., 123f

'Encounter-theology', 43ff
Evangelism, 9f, 28f
Evans, D. D., 47, 158f
Existentialism, 41ff
Experience (Religious), 40ff, 44ff, 46ff, 81ff

Faith, 68ff, 104
Fellowship, 88, 150f
Flew, R. N., 75, 85, 92
Forgiveness, 118ff
Forsyth, P. T., 161, 163, 166

George, A. R., 8, 45
Gospel, 86f, 101f, 122ff, 131f
Guilt, 115ff

Hazelton, R., 127
Healing, 4, 6f
Health, 26, 114f, 133ff
Hendry, G. S., 85, 120n, 122
Hiltner, S., 117f
Hodgson, L., 56, 61
Holiness, 72, 74ff
Holy Spirit, 59ff, 82f, 89f, 91f, 160
Hooft, W. A. V. 't, 92f

Image of God, 109f
Individualism, 27, 47, 77, 85f, 114, 145

Jesus, 8ff, 48f, 59, 73, 100, 115, 122, 159f
Johnson, P. E., 158ff
Jones, E., 134f
Justification, 68ff

Kelly, S. N. D., 35ff, 55
Kierkegaard, 42
Knowing, 42f, 176
Kraemer, Y., 143ff

Laity, 20, 143ff, 148ff
Language (Religious), 38ff
Law, 133ff
Lewis, C. S., 58, 65f, 149
Lindström, H., 12, 72
Love, 74ff, 176f
Lloyd-Jones, D. M., 46
Luther, M., 74, 122

McNeill, J. T., 4, 10, 14, 144
Means of Grace, 87f
Methodism, 20, 40f, 45f, 71f, 125, 152ff, 170ff
Micklem, E. R., 107
Ministers, 23ff, 144f, Chap. 11
Ministry, Chaps. 10 and 11
Mystery, 63f

Newbiggin, L., 63, 89

Oman, J., 111f
O'Neill, J. C., 49
Ordination, 152ff, 172f

Paterson, W. P., 168f
Paul, 14, 73, 123f
Perfection, 74ff
Pierce, C. A., 124
Prayer, see Worship
Preaching, 128ff, 156
Priesthood, 143ff

Providence, 127ff
Psychology and Psychiatry, 18f, 23ff, 59, 133ff, 150f
Psychosomatic, 5f, 133f

RESURRECTION, 139
Revelation, 38ff, 47f, 103f

SACRED, 107ff
Salvation, 12, Chap. 5, 122f, 136
Sanctification, 70ff, 74ff
Sayers, D., 58, 149
Secular, 107f
Shands, A. R., 148
Shepherd, 8f, Chap. 13
Sin, Chap. 8
Soul, 5ff
Spencer, I. S., 117f
Spiritual Direction, 20f, 23ff, 157ff, 174f
Stafford-Clark, D., 24f, 134

Suffering, 127ff

TELFER, W., 122n
Temple, W., 38, 95
Tennant F. R. 105n
Theology, 29f, Chap. 3, 54, 57f, 103ff, Chap. 12
Thurian M. 121
Tillich P. 132
Todd, J. M., 69
Trinity, Chap. 4

VIDLER, A., 92
Vriezen, Th. C., 5

WESLEY, J., 12f, 45f, 69, 70ff, 75f, 79ff, 157, 170f
White, E., 59
Wise, C. A., 47
Worship, 37, 65f, 108, 130, 147f

www.ingramcontent.com/pod-product-compliance
Lightning Source LLC
Chambersburg PA
CBHW071449150426
43191CB00008B/1287